WHY

Your *Child* Isn't Making the

GRADE

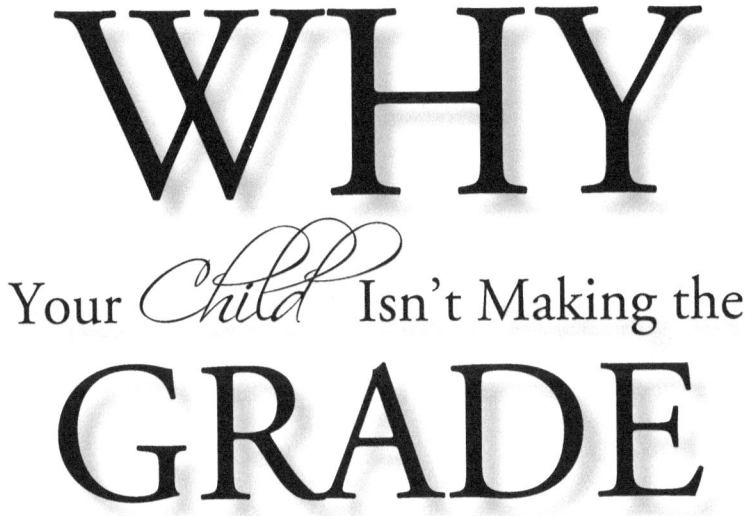

WHY

Your *Child* Isn't Making the

GRADE

ALTON MAXEL JAMES IV

authorHOUSE®

AuthorHouse™
1663 Liberty Drive
Bloomington, IN 47403
www.authorhouse.com
Phone: 1-800-839-8640

Published by AuthorHouse   11/19/2012

ISBN: 978-1-4772-8764-4 (sc)
ISBN: 978-1-4772-8763-7 (hc)
ISBN: 978-1-4772-8762-0 (e)

Library of Congress Control Number: 2012921133

This book is an honest account of many of the experiences that I have worked through. While I do express many personal beliefs and opinions on various matters, many ideas are supported by research and data. This book also takes into account the experiences of my colleagues that I worked with and with many that I did not. I engaged many educators in the formulation of this book—educators ranging in age, grades taught or administered, and years in education. All I ask is that you keep an open mind when reading this text and put it in perspective of your own educational experience, your community, and/or perhaps your current family, friends, or children.

Contents

My Education Background

My career in education began when I was still in high school. I attended an all-boys Catholic school; and during one's senior year, he had to perform what was called "Senior Service." In order to complete my senior service, I served as a teacher's assistant in a first grade classroom. I not only served as a sometimes facilitating co-teacher, but I also worked with students doing pull-outs (when a teacher takes a student out of the classroom to teach and tutor on a one-on-one basis). In addition to my service in the classroom, I exercised my talents as a musician in service to the school's students. Throughout this time, I led the students by playing and singing for their weekly Masses. When the school recognized this leadership, they put me in charge of planning their school music programs on different occasions for all grades [PreK-8].

When I completed high school and my first year of college at the University of Michigan—Ann Arbor, I worked as a course assistant for a freshman English College Writing course. Essentially, I was an undergraduate G.S.I. (Graduate Student Instructor). This position allowed me to cultivate my skills and abilities as an instructor and mentor (considering I had to work with the students outside of class as well). Following this experience, I decided to apply for a Peer Adviser position for the following summer term. The role called for me to not only be a resident adviser, but I also instructed a college readiness course.

These various experiences inspired me to study the nuances of education on a macro level; therefore, I enrolled in a K12 Administration and Policy Master's Degree Program (again U of M Ann Arbor). While studying, I immersed myself in two different teaching roles. I became a substitute teacher at the elementary school where I served as a TA—additionally, I taught a speech course at a small proprietary college (it was a course requirement for all of the disciplines offered). The coupled experiences of teaching and researching provided great insight into the interplay of student outcomes over the breath of the PreK-16 spectrum. Most importantly, I benefited from the first-hand experience of analyzing the factors that hinder and/or drive student achievement.

Upon graduation in June 2010, I joined an alternative teaching certification program. I immediately left for Chicago to undergo my training and teach summer school on the Southside. Unfortunately, through student and staff discussions, we discovered that half of my summer school students were in gangs. One fourth of them were drug users. Three were drug dealers. Of these twenty high school students, not one was a proficient reader. Three were at a middle school reading level. The remaining students read below a fifth grade level. The lowest student read on a beginning first grade level-struggling to read standard three-letter words.

The following two years consisted of me teaching 6th and 7th grade English Language Arts—one at a first year charter school—the second at an established and highly touted Blue Ribbon School (a prestigious award given to high achieving schools). Again, I gained the invaluable experience of experiencing the dichotomy of drastically different schools. Furthermore, each required a great deal of my own time and leadership. I held a multitude of roles: spearheading a study skills class, a remediation class for retention students, a financial literacy class, a piano and voice class, a school spelling bee, a student vs. staff basketball game, amongst a plethora of other initiatives.

Beyond these initiatives, I have served in other key critical areas: curriculum developer, faculty chair for a school improvement team, and a faculty chair for the National Junior Honors Society. Among all of the other initiatives and community partnerships created and proposed to leadership, I cannot recall the myriad of other opportunities that I was instrumental in spawning on a day to day basis. At this point in my educational career, I am pursuing an Education Specialist and a PhD in Higher Education Administration at Wayne State University. My ultimate goal will be to enhance the matriculation rates of black males from secondary to post-secondary institutions. It is an overwhelming struggle that plagues the very success of our country as it stands today. Lastly, I am currently working as a college readiness counselor and instructing choir, college writing, and African American History.

Chapter 1: Denigrated Demographics

Nuclear Family

One of the most under-analyzed and oversimplified issues in contemporary society is the nature of demographics. The first problem of note in regards to demographics rests in the degradation of the nuclear family. For years, strong marriages and households have been the pillar of American Society. Religious institutions frequently suggest that the "First Church" a child receives is found in the household—from a strong nuclear family. As religious institutions insist on having parents teach the values and morals that are necessary to pursue a healthy faith life, the same devices are needed in order to have children enter school eager and ready to learn. However, with the shifts that we are seeing in divorce rates as well as teen pregnancy, the face of the nuclear family has taken a dramatic turn for the worse. Statistics and studies prove time and time again that children benefit from the security of a stable household—a benefit that bodes well in terms of the health of a child: physically, mentally, and emotionally.

Undoubtedly, there is a tragic correlation between the increased rates we continue to see in debilitating health issues in our children today and educational success—health issues like autism, obesity, ADD,

ADHD, as well a whole host of other illnesses. Almost every facet of humanity requires a support system to accomplish any monumental task. There is an old adage that says, "It takes a village to raise a child." While this is absolutely true, we also lose sight of the importance of the "First Village" that a child is exposed to in the first place—the home. In an era when the "Fast Life" is glorified through American media and divorces are as commonplace as when one changes his or her shoes, we set up our children to assume they have no support systems. If the adults in a child's life show no consistency, what hope does a child have for stability in his or her own life?

Ultimately, a shift must occur in the psyche of this country if we are to make significant changes with our students. A committed home of two adults must be glorified in our media and our communities to begin to allow strong nuclear families to become a reality once more. Additionally, we must see parents have their children at ages when they have secured a career and a means to raise their children. Although teen pregnancy rates have declined in recent years, a detrimental problem still exists with parents having children "too early," without commitment to one another, and without the physical, emotional, and financial well-being to do so properly. As controversial as the term family planning has become in society, on some level, people need to genuinely find legitimate means to plan the appropriate time in their lives to raise children.

Birth Control

As it relates to family planning, the advent of birth control has created a huge shift in the nature of how society functions. However, by no means am I saying that birth control is a reason for the plight of education today. What I am going to illustrate is how its proliferation in today's world has altered some sects of society in ways that indirectly negatively influence educational outcomes. Firstly, the introduction of birth control came along during the same era as the signing of the G.I. Bill (a bill that created incentives for military vets and "non-traditional" students of the time to enter colleges and universities). This is important to note because of two reasons: one, we saw a shift in the American industry.

This shift in America's industry made the acquisition of jobs contingent upon attaining degrees from higher education institutions. Furthermore, it essentially started the eradication of the middle class. Once people could not rely on high school diplomas to create a meaningful and productive life, the floodgates were opened to increasing the cost of higher education as well as decreasing access to it. When industry moved away from agriculture and manufacturing, we ushered in an era in which only a select few jobs are available to a small minority of qualified individuals. This leads us to our second note of importance. In conjunction with the institution of birth control, a different climate was created in society. Birth control empowered women to take control of family planning in a way that had never been done before. Consequently, women were enabled to enter the workforce more easily and pursue careers in ways that wouldn't be possible without the worry of starting or adding to a family.

Coupled with laws spawning, protecting, and continuing affirmative action, women began their rise in educational attainment in staggering fashion. Given this shift in American households to having two adults working, the cost of living rose dramatically (not that women entering the workforce created this trend) along with the necessity of having a two-parent working household. Despite the greatness in the garnering of rights and educational attainment that has benefited women since this epoch, a definite decline in the nuclear family has ensued (rise in divorce rates, rise in teenage pregnancy [ironically], and the rise of unwed mothers). I'm not suggesting that these factors are a direct result of the rise in rights and educational attainment; however, there is an ironic correlation nonetheless.

Isolation

In retrospectively analyzing the start of America and its cultural progression, a recurring motif of exclusivity arises in its chronology. Although America was supposed to be built on religious freedom, people quickly learned of this "ideal" facade. Very soon, people realized that only Christianity was truly recognized or deemed legitimate. This notion was clear when American settlers felt that they needed to evangelize and save the Native Americans from their "barbarous paganism." Moving further, Americans felt the need to essentially eradicate the Native American population through their own barbarous genocide—a genocide that isolated Americans away from others—an isolation that forced Native Americans to the outskirts of America on reservations or to Canada. Eventually, Americans found a way to isolate themselves from the Chinese, Irish, Jewish, Blacks, and any other minorities that did not fit the "American W.A.S.P. (White Anglo-Saxon Protestant)" image. I highlight this of particular importance because of what this mindset has done to the fabric of American communities.

Specifically, the race riots of the 50s, 60s, and 70s created permanent ghettos and underclass communities. On the other hand, the suburban sprawl during this era contributed to specific racial and ethnic groups being stratified amongst American metropolises. This suburban sprawl left historically disenfranchised communities to their own devices without economic security, access to decently waged jobs, or access to post-secondary institutions. The damage that legal segregation posed to the American economy has been far-reaching and quite detrimental; however, this damage pales in comparison to the destructive force of self-segregation (one that was created due to "White Flight" and the suburban sprawl [the time following the many race riots during the 50s and 60s that spurred vast numbers of White citizens to move from urban centers]). Unfortunately, recent studies have shown that this phenomenon continues to this day with groups choosing to live in communities with certain racial and economic makeups.

Until our communities can become more heterogeneous along the lines of race and class, students will suffer due to the lack of diversity and economic stability to their school funding. Furthermore, racial, cultural, and economic diversity bodes well for the overall safety, management, and economic health of a community. These factors are critical in harboring positive feelings—factors that produce emotionally healthy children that are ready to be productive students.

Concentrated Capitalism

With the aforementioned harmful effects of isolation in society, the economic downfall of society has become exacerbated greatly. It goes without saying that one of the staples of American society rests in the notion of the free enterprise system and capitalism (arguably venture or "vulture" capitalism). Despite the original intention of creating a society that rewards the hardworking, we have now come to a period when "equal-opportunity" is one evil punch line. Our society is now predicated on "Conspicuous Consumption," and what I like to call

"Capitalism on Steroids." Phrases like "Keeping up with the Jones" have plagued American communities on epic proportions. With credit card, medical bill, home, and student loan debt at dangerous highs, American families are crippled under the weight of today's capitalistic market. Now more than ever, the projected educational attainment of a child can be predicted based solely on the income of the household. Additionally, the previously mentioned factor of the strength of the nuclear family plays a great deal in the educational success of a child as well.

Due to the fact that households of greater incomes typically live in affluent communities, they have a larger tax base; and consequently, they have more money being allocated to their children's schools. Families of greater wealth have the means to donate time, money, and resources to their children's schools (outside of their tax contributions). Due to the lack of revenue sharing amongst school districts, there will always be school systems that perennially lack the resources to adequately educate their students. In looking back to the notion of our debt driven society, government programs and systems continue to be in the "red" in terms of budgets. Unfortunately, the story is no different when it comes to school systems. However, beyond the ramifications of dwindling dollars to schools, our calamity with concentrated capitalism has greater and more widespread effects than this. Because Americans are suffering from large amounts of debt, American families will be more strapped and strained as a result.

With the overwhelming number of single parent households and the skyrocketed numbers of unemployment, how will families manage to provide a stable household for children to feel secure and primed to learn? With so many Americans being underemployed, how will our children maintain hope for a brighter future for themselves? With a decrease in home ownership as a result of the job and housing markets, success rates for our students look grim. Research and studies have shown that home ownership is a positive factor in children succeeding in their studies. In spite of the fact that American society is predicated on the premise of capitalism, there has to be some point at which equal-opportunity is a reality; and, we must see that economically disenfranchised populations cannot sustain this economy—in all actuality, America as a whole cannot sustain. What is an advanced country that has an overwhelming majority of its members struggling? As Adam Smith once said, "No society can surely be happy of which the far greater part of the members are poor and miserable." As we say that a happy worker is a productive worker, a happy student is a productive student!

Chapter 2: Social Capital

Lack of Access

A glaring problem in the success of our students falls on the grounds of a lack of social capital. Considering the advantages to individuals whom benefit from America's concentrated capitalism, these individuals are privy to a parcel of society that provides privilege and power. It is noted from several sources that the top 1% of earners in America control the vast majority of America's wealth. In a system in which people thrive from overt patronage and nepotism, how can one expect our students to have a feeling of empowerment to better his or her place in society? The notion of being upwardly mobile has been contorted and twisted in the reality of how our economy actually functions. Keeping this in mind, as a society, we must find ways to provide access to social capital. This may sound next to impossible, but think of the implications of having people of all backgrounds and socioeconomic statuses to be privy to privileges held typically to the wealthy.

In understanding how to navigate higher education institutions, professional settings, and influential social settings, all people would be elevated to function in realms that typically only benefit the affluent. As many professionals understand, it is not always about how much education one has received that creates success. In many cases, it boils down to whom one is in association with, networking, and intangibles (such as charisma, cultural knowledge, and proper etiquette). If we are to build an entire nation ready to take on 21st century technological careers that must function in a global economy, we will never reach our full potential if everyone does not have intimate knowledge of different ways of life and access to social capital.

Lack of Exposure

As it stands, similar to issues in access, many of our students lack the baseline exposure needed to capitalize on the access he or she may have. When one looks to our more impoverished or disenfranchised communities, many of the foundations of social capital are missing in these communities. For example, many of our urban cities, or metropolises for that matter, lack history museums, art museums, theaters, music halls, sophisticated libraries, community centers, or community-significant places of worship. These institutions provide people with a level of exposure to many of the things the world has to offer. In order to capitalize on the benefits of social capital, people must be primed and poised to function in such important professional settings. Consider this—many of our professional organizations now hold corporate functions around formal dinner parties and golf outings. These types of venues require the cultural and etiquette knowledge to even begin to sufficiently involve one's self in professional environments. Our students are greatly suffering due to the fact that they are not being exposed to different aspects of society that will allow them to make meaningful connections to other subject matters when in school.

It has been empirically illustrated that people retain information at a greater rate when he or she can attach new learning to previous experiences and background knowledge. However, when students lack the exposure to other realms of life, they will be hindered in their ability to create new learning opportunities for themselves. With that being said, I would argue that our nation overlooks our most precious piece of social capital that exists—our language. Language is but the means to meaning and the very vehicle that facilitates communication and disseminates knowledge to the masses. Studies indicate that the number one measure in determining a child's success in school is the number of vocabulary words that one has in his or her personal lexicon. When a child has the knowledge of a great number of words, he or she can make connections in ways that eases the acquisition of newer words. Furthermore, these students usually enter school with a more advanced understanding of syntax and semantics that allows for a more fluid learning experience across all subject matters.

Consider this—most minority students are entering school knowing at least 50% less vocabulary then their Caucasian counterparts. In taking into account decades, if not eons, of segregation, terrorism, poor education, disenfranchisement, as well as a whole host of other social slights, these setbacks have become generational inheritances. Given that we have groups that have created their own vernacular or colloquial rhetoric as counterculture or in-group culture building, it detracts from a student's ability to flourish in an English based curriculum. Furthermore, we have ESL (English as a Second Language) students and first-generation American students now more than ever. If we are to see significant improvements in our educational outcomes, we must provide students early and continuous access to significant social capital throughout their educational careers.

Social Expectations

It seems as if the debate between nature vs. nurture has been happening for forever. The debate calls into question whether or not people are more products of their genes or the environments in which they mature. One thing science has proven is that people definitely are influenced by their environments and the experiences that they undergo. When one looks at the landscape of America and the makeup of different regions, states, and cities, we can see stark variances between differing areas. In delving into their specific nuances, many communities have a history of high rates of unemployment, illiteracy, drug abuse, alcoholism, teen pregnancy, incarceration, homelessness, etc. Considering environments have profound effects on individuals, many young students don't possess the "role models" or environments that encourage educational success. In an era when "Reality T.V." is glorified amongst other media that glamorizes discord and "drama" in society, these mindsets become engrained in our young students.

Given this premise, certain communities almost expect its young people to be future teen parents, drug users, dealers, prisoners, or "dead beats." Educational theorists have proposed that students typically work best when they receive 4 or 5 positive remarks versus every one piece of negative feedback. Taking this ratio into account, it seems rather impossible for students in these areas to internalize feelings of confidence, hope, motivation, or sentiments of success. It can almost be predicted that people, in general, will strive to meet the expectations cast before them. If negative, then people can fulfill that prophecy in devastating fashion. However, when looking toward fulfilling positive expectations, even if a student doesn't reach the highest, they are still reaching toward positive achievement. Ultimately, that is the greatest thing we can ask of a society—to constantly be striving toward self-improvement. Conversely, when one looks to how society actually functions, we see a vastly different picture. Every community must have resounding expectations of college graduation, committed and loving households, family planning, and life-long learning and improvement. Only then can we begin to see the cultural and psychological shifts that will be necessary to properly facilitate student achievement that is grounded in the positive expectations of every community.

Negative Social Circles

Similar to the previous section outlining social expectations, one's social circle has a profound effect on the projected educational outcome of a student. Unfortunately, it appears that the "media" makes minority or urban successes to be anomalies that are almost impossible to replicate. At the end of the day, these individuals were subject to the confines and social limitations of their communities and environments. Regardless of whether or not minority students are the focal point of a discussion, all students are in some fashion are subject to the influence of their social atmosphere. Particularly, research reveals how many affluent communities are seeing rising numbers of students using drugs and alcohol in binge fashion. Additionally, across the country, we are losing vast numbers of students to social circles that are wrapped around cliques, gangs, and (ironically) video games. Our students are creating subcultures that counter the established norms of behaviors that are conducive for educational success and growth.

As our society morphs into a world in which we have access to the ideas and thoughts of individuals on a second-by-second basis, we run the risk of living out our lives in public. This tight line becomes dangerous when exclusive circles or personal information becomes public knowledge and public debate. Ultimately, these polarizing aspects of today's social circles detract from the learning environment. Just a few years ago, before the advent of cell phones and the internet, socialization played more of a backseat role to education; however, today, the minute-to-minute happenings of students' lives become the focus in and outside of the school. Essentially, society, and the values that it holds, (or rather lack there-of) becomes a mitigating force in the advancement of our educational system as it stands today. Our social circles must shift to being centered on common goals and efforts for self-improvement if we are to see a trickle-down effect in our homes, schools, and communities at large.

Chapter 3: Economic Capital

Community Schools

Bluntly, urban schools (traditionally majority minority) receive significantly less money than their suburban counterparts. This harkens back to the previous discussion on the section in Chapter 1 dedicated to the notion of concentrated capitalism. The dollar allocation to schools is determined by some or all of these factors based on the state, city, or local community in which one lives: state taxes, city taxes, or a local millage (property tax). The more affluent a community is the more dollars its schools will receive. Moreover, schools receive a certain per-pupil expenditure (a specified amount of money for each student that is enrolled in the school). Recently, there has been a huge trend of students attempting to leave urban areas and expand to the suburbs or surrounding communities. This movement leaves communities with decimated numbers in terms of student bodies—additionally, these communities are left with more impoverished people with a very small tax base. Therefore, a great number of minority communities are plagued with little resources being pumped into its schools due to a lack of a strong tax base. The level of impropriety that exists due to this inequality is unconstitutional.

Although power to conduct public schooling is delegated to state governments, it is unconstitutional for schools to be separate and/or unequal. Given the information presented in the section on isolation, it is clear that the current state of education is quite separate and quite unequal. Tangentially, our country has been known for its fanatic following of sports such as football and basketball. Even our cherished NFL and NBA leagues run on a system known as revenue sharing. This system creates a standard that every team will have the same amount of money to spend on hiring players for their teams. Granted, players then have a choice as to what team he may wish to play for (some teams have some secondary or tertiary advantages over the other); however, each team starts on an equal playing field. How great would it be if every student in this country accounted for the same amount of money going to his or her school? At that point, it would simply be a matter of choice as to what school the student and their families wanted to attend. This system would cultivate an environment in which competition would make schools rise to the occasion and flourish.

A form of healthy capitalism could emerge and bring about an era when all schools would have an adequate amount of resources to accomplish the necessary tasks at hand. As previously outlined, schools are funded and regulated by their local governments. In reverting back and assessing the demographic make-up of American communities, many metropolises are segregated in terms of race, socioeconomic status, and ethnicity. Granted, segregation of any form is realized today as negative; however, the true destruction of segregation usually gets lost in the discussion of race and rights. Higher education institutions frequently harp on the idea that diversity is an essential part of their learning environments. They argue that diversity adds to the learning environment in ways that allow students to be exposed to various ideas and experiences.

Many college freshmen experience what is known as a "culture shock." It is the overwhelming and uncomfortable feeling of being outside of one's comfort zone due to being around different people with different backgrounds and beliefs. The experience of being immersed in many cultures and ideas proves to be an extremely important and formative time in one's life. But, why should only a minority of young adults have this experience? When looking at the history of America, one can see the many struggles that have come at the expense of race, religion, sex, sexual orientation, ethnicity, height, mental acuity, political ideals, land ownership, gender, and age, as well as a whole host of other identifiers. Historically, Americans have been very xenophobic—wars and struggles have been waged in the name of these factors.

With that being said, the shape and make-up of our communities are doing our students a huge injustice because they are being sheltered. Yes, families have some ability to allow or hinder exposure; but, by the shear nature of whom or where one may be, he or she has almost inherited a predetermined set of cultural exposures. If we are to mitigate the biases and prejudices that plague our society, it must begin with the diversification of our community schools. We live in an ever more globalized world, yet we live in ever more isolated bubbles. Beyond changing the nature of how diverse bodies of people interact and behave, the educational future of our students depends on the diversification of our neighborhoods and schools.

Mental State

The mindset of individuals plays a key role in the economic makeup of a community. As mentioned before, we have become a nation driven by debt. One can see that correlation in looking at how individual households are in the red, as well as cities and states, and for the entire federal government that sits with trillions of dollars in debt. In some regards, Americans not only possess an attitude of "Keeping up with the Jones," but they also hold fast to the problem of attempting to live outside one's means. We are seeing an unprecedented time of young adults still living at home, low rates of home ownership, high rates of renting, and increased numbers of the homeless. At a time when pensions are becoming a dinosaur of the forgotten past, we now rely on personal savings and 401ks to ensure our financial futures. In reality, most Americans are unable to or fail to take advantage of these economic security measures. Financial experts suggest that one's income should be divided into three equal spending partitions—1/3 should be saved, 1/3 should go to living expenses, and another 1/3 should go to all other expenses. However, it seems as though we've reached a time when conventional wisdom is cast out the window. As a personal testimony, I cannot recall the number of people that I've encountered that are struggling financially yet own pricey gadgets, dazzling automobiles or wardrobe accessories, or go on lavish trips.

Again, it all goes back to the collective consciousness and mindset of our society. In an era of accelerating technology and the sense of entitlement and luxury, Americans are spending money quite irresponsibly in comparison to previous generations that lived much more modestly. Granted, the cost of living has risen in conjunction with inflation; however, many Americans are making more money today yet they do not save as much as previous generations. Although France is a much different society than the one the U.S. functions under, the French have developed a society in which they do not live lavishly; although, they have found a means to ensure the economic stability of their people—a stability that trickles down through every facet of their society (including education). The aforementioned sections illustrate how the economic landscape of society plays out in the success of our educational system. Yet, the actual psychology of society as it pertains to the economy does not support the educational system. My meaning rests in the idea of where people actually spend their money—not their ideas about education.

It can be deduced that the priorities of a society can be revealed through where money is spent and allocated. In regards to American expenditures, outside of living expenses, an overwhelming majority of our dollars are attributed to "vanity costs." In other words, we disproportionately spend money on entertainment, personal beautification, social media, and luxury items. Essentially, our expenditures reflect a need to cater to a sense of laziness and personally indulgent behavior. If our collective consciousness reflects a need to play to our need to "escape," then we'll never ascend to the level of creating a society predicated on advancement. I look at the following elements of our recent history as dangerous indicators: the advent and rise of plastic surgery, Botox, social media, Reality T.V., the debate on the legalization of marijuana, recreational drugs, video games and multimedia, steroids and other performance enhancing drugs, Viagra, etc. Our spending reveals a need to escape from reality, stroke our egos, and cater to our self-centered needs. When our society reaches a juncture of focusing outwardly, then we will begin to see our priorities center on things that evolve humanity and not the individual—i.e., valuing education, learning, and growth.

Family Business

The idea of family businesses has been somewhat of a founding principle of familial sustenance. The entrepreneurial spirit has been one that has guided many Americans to grand success. Unfortunately, these "legitimate" businesses and successes have come from a multitude of sources but to only white families (usually). We typically refer to these large corporations as being from "Old Money." These industries include slavery (plantations), oil, transportation, and manufacturing. With today's shift to the technological, these old forms of money are virtually impossible to infiltrate without familial ties. Ironically, the racial and economic makeup of our technological industries looks somewhat similar today. In moving forward and assessing the nature of businesses today, the overwhelming majority of start-up businesses fail shortly after their inceptions. Historically, children that are raised in family businesses have ease of access to social capital as well as great educational systems—not to mention, a guaranteed career that will be sustaining and profitable when handed the reins to the family business. It is overwhelmingly dangerous to see the lack of home ownership as well as ownership of a personal enterprise. In contemporary times, we are seeing businesses frequently fail, pensions evaporate, and benefits dwindle. This creates a much larger unemployed worker pool, a shrinkage in job availability, and a level of under-employment for those holding jobs.

At this juncture, we are left with a series of glaring issues. First, businesses must cease patronage and nepotism, or reinvest its profits into benefits for their employees (in conjunction with a more evenly distributed salary schedule). Secondly, businesses must make concerted efforts to be more open in their hiring practices (i.e., ceasing the use of internal job postings or other measures that make it difficult to obtain employment), or businesses must invest in their own employees through measures that increase training and ensure lifetime careers. We are at a point now when the average worker changes jobs or careers several times throughout their working lives. This level of instability and turnover within industries only decreases the potential productivity of an organization while increasing the level of frustration and anxiety from employees. Workers must feel confident in their work performance as well as job security if we are to see positive changes in our work force as well as students. What level of success can we expect from our students when they live in a world in which we have vast unemployment and high attrition rates in employment? Students will begin to not see the benefit of exploring their educations when they see no meaningful gains in its procurement. The reshaping of American industry practices must undergo revolution if it is to be a conduit of student interest and success in education.

Legacy

One of the biggest and most important aspects of the human condition rests in the notion that we have a fixed—a finite existence. We are born. And then we die. Humanity continues to drive forward in thought and technology because we annually pass down our knowledge to the next generation. And in my opinion, knowledge is the most valuable commodity that we can leave behind outside of morality. Despite the fact that the globalization of our world has facilitated the dissemination of information from generation to generation, we are failing miserably at passing down economic capital—wealth, money, resources, etc. As apparent as the media has made the crisis of college affordability, we repeatedly see tuition hikes each year as college debt climbs ever higher. Granted, securing funds without debt for our students would be an endeavor that would aid all Americans; this gift of legacy would only be the beginning.

So often, "Reality T.V." and other brands of media peer into the worlds of the rich and famous. Many of these families bequeath trusts and other forms of wealth to their children. These young adults have the ability to thrive because they have aid in the purchases of their first cars, homes, weddings, etc. These parts of one's life can be difficult to manage and budget; however, when a young student can focus on his or her studies and the procurement of good employment, he or she has the means to secure a solid career that will be conducive to sufficiently raising the next generation of students. If executed properly with the best family planning at hand, a young person will have the facilities to have a stable career that will lend itself to a secure nuclear family.

As a society, we must get into the habit of being legacy focused. We must adhere to the idea that saving is more important than spending—that delayed gratification is what drives success, innovation, and above all, joy. I cannot tell one how many students lack the appreciation for delayed gratification. I would argue that the majority of students today simply "go-through-the-motions" in school—students today are overwhelmingly lazy (a point that will be expounded upon in the following chapters). If we are to change the face of education, we must undoubtedly change the nature of adults in this country. The goal of handing down the appreciation for hard work and delayed gratification must be a staple of raising families.

Technology has afforded us the privilege of receiving things at almost instantaneous rates as compared to previous generations. In spite of these accomplishments, we must not lose the wisdom in the core of the "American Dream." Although its validity and application to all people are questioned, the notion of working hard to provide a life for one's family is to be commended. And ultimately, a part of that dream must involve what can be bestowed as a legacy. In building the American family, we not only build education, but we secure a future for our students and our children.

Chapter 4: Health

Physical Aptitude

It seems as if one cannot turn on a television without hearing discussions about the obesity crisis in America. From advertisements from the NFL to the First Lady giving presentations, the level of health consciousness has been raised in recent times. However, Americans are notorious for having very poor habits in terms of health. Statistically, we are known for a lack of consistent exercise and wise food choices. But, I think we need to take this premise a step further. The way in which we cultivate crops and raise livestock has come into question. The use of pesticides on crops and hormones to "fatten-up" livestock have caused great controversy. Ultimately, the way in which we process and preserve food pose great risk to our health. In conjunction with food choices and a lack of exercise, we have to look to what our society is doing to our environment.

With deforestation and the proliferation of carbon emissions, we are degrading more than just our breathable air. We are destroying our atmosphere and the ozone that protects us. As our protection fails, we increase the amount of radiation and other harmful particles that enter our atmosphere. Various forms of radiation are known to cause severe health problems—mainly, cancer. Although this may be a more far-reaching health risk that does not directly influence our students, diet and exercise habits do. Currently, we are overwhelmed with the number of autistic, diabetic, asthmatic, obese, and ADD (attention deficit disorder) students now more than ever before. These physical ailments have real consequences in the classroom. When one's body is not in proper form, the mind cannot perform adequately. Therefore, the toll the body takes leads to the mental gaps we see in our students.

Mental Aptitude

If one believes the physical health of our students is out of control, the same can be said of the mental health as well. Test scores around the nation are absolutely abysmal, and yet cut scores are being raised. Ironically, these measures are being instituted in an era when, again, students are being diagnosed with an array of mental disabilities. Additionally, educators are seeing a spike in the number of students referred for special education services, IEPs (Individualized Education Plans), and 504 plans (another variation of individualized plans). Why are we continually seeing a brain drain in our students? Of course, the factors above play a great deal in the regression in intellectual competence. However, essentially, we can look no further than how unprepared our students go into school with significantly less vocabulary than he or she should possess. In the end, a student's mental abilities are a result of every step from prenatal care to early childhood development. A combination of a suitable home and community environment plays a significant role in ensuring a child is mentally stable and prepared to enter the school environment. Only when a child has the mental and social faculties can he or she successfully navigate the waters of the educational system.

Emotional Aptitude

One may assume that the discussion of emotional stability could be wrapped up in a dialogue pertaining to a student's mental state. In actuality, a student's emotional aptitude rests in not only their mentality, but also in their environments. Similar to the rise in special education referrals, many students are now being sent to counselors and social workers on grounds of being emotionally impaired. It is absolutely devastating to educational success to be plagued by emotional issues. One cannot fully focus on one's studies when he or she has trouble with their emotional stability. In my experience in the urban environment, many students suffered from homelessness, parental instability (in terms of presence and employment), physical, sexual, and emotional abuse, drug and alcohol abuse, poverty, hunger, and even verbal abuse. These detriments weigh heavy on a person (especially a child). As banal as it may sound, as a society, we must actually change the way in which we build children and address them. Our young students need to experience a great sense of love in their households. Students need parental, physical, mental, and emotional stability to be ready to take on the challenges of a classroom. Period.

Longevity

As science and medicine progresses in innovation, we expect our society to become healthier and benefit from longer lives. While life expectancy is rising on average, we still see a multitude of ailments that are threatening the quality of life for many Americans—lung disease, heart disease, obesity, diabetes, etc. Ultimately, our failing health care system continuously poses great risk to our students today. In an era of ever-growing medical procedures, America still has one of the worst health care systems that does not provide care to all of its citizens. If the Constitution expresses that everyone has the right to life, liberty, and the pursuit of happiness, then the country must provide the right to life to its citizens in the form of health care. When one analyzes communities of different socioeconomic statuses, then one will see a glaring disparity between the life expectancies between those who are poor and more affluent. As outlined before, students cannot be successful when they have health problems to overcome. These problems can be any combination of physical, mental, or emotional. As a nation, we cannot stand by and allow for the life expectancy to merely be a function of race and class. When people are subject to particular expectations of a quality of health and life, it has direct implications for the level of motivation an individual will have in life.

If one foresees a life of poor health and complications, what would be a motivating factor for pursuing tasks for one's own edification like education? As a country, we must ensure that all citizens have the same access to health care at no out-of-pocket cost to the patient. We cannot sustain a nation, or expect it grow, if its citizens have to make choices as to what to pay for when it comes to health. Although, Americans do need to make much better choices in terms of diet and exercise habits. However, we cannot expect schools to provide this health care to students, just as we cannot expect students to be stressed about cost and receiving a quality education. And yes, I am referring to the costs of higher education. If a student is juggling working, loans, and other stressful measures just to earn a degree, are they really learning at their best and fulfilling their highest potential? We must remove the roadblocks that hinder our students from learning if we are to truly ascend to, and transcend, the educational excellence of our educational counterparts—mainly, Finland and China.

Chapter 5: Over-Emphasis on Data

Formative Assessments

Educators utilize two types of assessments: formative and summative. Formative assessments are meant to be used as assessments that illustrate how much a student is learning. Essentially, they are not meant to be graded; but rather, they are meant for a teacher to see how students are learning and to improve their teaching based on the results. Formative assessments are effective tools at seeing how a class is or is not sufficiently learning the lessons being taught. In relation to how lessons are derived and taught, effectively utilizing formative assessments becomes a daunting task. Not saying that it can't be done, but one must take into account how much a teacher is actually expected to teach during a given year. The states have historically issued which educational standards students should learn over the course of a year. The number of standards range from dozens up to around one hundred. This may sound rather small; however, each standard involves teaching a whole host of smaller objectives that allows a student to fully learn the standard.

For example (not a direct example but stated simply for understanding), a standard may say, "The student will understand the styles, elements, and structures of poetry." This may appear to be straight to the point. But, one has to think about what each of those aspects entails. There are an enumerable amount of styles: limerick, haiku, sonnet, acrostic, ballad, etc. (there are dozens upon dozens of types). Ultimately, an educator is left to determine which ones to teach and how much time to delegate to each. Furthermore, when looking at the elements, there are many elements of poetry as well: personification, alliteration, rhyme, assonance, consonance, onomatopoeia, etc. (the list goes on and on). Then, in terms of structure, the list is inexhaustible as well: quatrains, stanzas, iambic pentameter, syllabication, etc. In education, we are frequently bombarded with a long list of things to teach and few resources to do the job. While formative assessments are critical in giving important feedback to a teacher in how his or her students are learning, the amount of time is too small to assess true learning. With many class periods consisting of less than an hour, that leaves little time to teach a lesson and allow students to practice. In our desire to have constant feedback on student performance, we run this risk of testing more than teaching.

Summative Assessments

If the desire to have regular feedback on student performance isn't daunting enough, the pressure created by summative assessments is absolutely overwhelming. Summative assessments reflect what a student has learned in order to grade them or attribute a certain level of learning to that student. These are found as tests, exams, or standardized tests (state, federal, or national tests). At the school level, tests and exams are school or teacher provided tests at the end of chapters, units, or semesters. While these are necessary to see what a student has learned, their use becomes gruesome at best. I describe it as such due to the pressures that are created from standardized tests. Schools are funded and ranked based on their students' performance on state, federal, or national tests. Unfortunately, these tests are mostly given in the form of multiple-choice and are designed in fashions that test more of test-taking skills rather than the content itself. With strict time constraints on these assessments, we are essentially cramming in test time and testing students more on their mental fortitude rather than their natural abilities, knowledge, and understanding.

I am fully aware that testing and data is necessary to know where a student is performing; however, when as a nation we test in this manner, we fail to obtain an accurate picture of where our students fall in terms of achievement. On a personal note, I cannot even begin to recall the number of students that informed me that they "just clicked some answers," or "didn't read a passage," or "just glanced over" the information or questions. A large number of students have reached the point where they are apathetic about test-taking and don't see the importance or the weight they carry. Unfortunately, with the dwindling number of students that are actively invested in their educations, those students seem to care more about their personal GPAs and other matters that affect them personally. With that being said, they make sure they perform on standardized tests that help their own personal cause (a high school placement test or ACT exam). In overemphasizing the importance of all tests and over-testing, we essentially take away the desire to perform.

I see the experience as being analogous to prohibition that took place in the early 20th century. The allure of alcohol was at a high peak during prohibition. Clubs and social scenes had to operate covertly as people were engrossed in the social life around alcohol consumption. However, at the end of prohibition, society lost its overwhelming desire for the experience of alcohol. Granted, people still indulge a great deal in alcohol and long for the social aspect of it as well. However, imagine how something that is already very popular could lose some of its intrigue when it is actually legalized! Although it may seem impossible to equate prohibition to test taking, students truly lose a sense of investment in the test-taking process because it has lost the esoteric prestige that they once held. Testing shouldn't be this overly utilized thing that we throw in kids' faces—testing needs to be spaced out in a sense where children have the desire to see where they truly stand academically.

Test Alignment

In regards to the issues raised in terms of formative and summative assessments, the problem of test alignment comes into play. Test alignment refers to tests having the same information presented in the same fashion as it was taught. So often now, teachers teach in vastly different ways than other examinations actually assess. The lack of coherence between the presentation of content in lessons and the following of that content on assessments is a glaring issue in education. In fact, we've reached a point where educators wind up in the unfortunate position of needing to focus on the standardized test. Educators refer to this phenomenon as "teaching to the test." Although this may seem a wise decision in order to procure the desired test results from students, the tests themselves aren't structured in a fashion that assesses true mastery of content. As previously discussed, examinations typically test test-taking skills as well as random reading abilities.

Unfortunately, these skills are assessed in a vacuum and are not directly correlative to the manner in which they were taught. We cannot continue to have a disconnection between how we teach and how we assess students. There should be total transparency between each aspect of testing. There should not be any surprises for our students and what they will be required to do and know on an exam. When we get to the point of taking away the fear in testing, we will enable our students to relax and be excited about showing what they know. The future of American Education depends on it.

Relevance

"What's the point?"

I would be remiss if I even attempted to recall how many times I have heard a student say this remark about a test. And many times, I have to agree—what is the point? When tests don't actually measure a student's knowledge of subject matter, then why have subject specific tests? We can't expect a student to take an assessment seriously when it has no bearing on what they have actually experienced in a classroom. Beyond that, students frequently remark that school and external assessments fail to matter in terms of their future careers and aspirations. Ultimately, tests and exams must reflect real-world scenarios if students are to realize the true value of education and assessments. They must be able to understand and use education as a tool and not a goal to reach. It must be an ongoing journey—a vehicle to pursuing personal goals while contributing to society as a meaningful and productive citizen.

Chapter 6: Emphasis on Classroom and Not Experiential Learning

Cultural Relevance

One of the hot topic terms in education these days is "Cultural Relevance." Cultural relevance refers to an exam or classroom content being relevant to the socioeconomic, racial, or ethnic group that the test is being given to. Whenever I think about this topic, I cannot help but think about the education movie *Lean on Me*. In one scene the camera goes over the shoulder of a student as she is taking a test. The question she is currently on says something to the effect of: "Billy has a breakfast consisting of eggs, toast, and orange juice." The answers provide options like: "strange, ordinary, crazy, and blue." To the dismay of the principal, the student chose the option "strange." Whereas this example is hyperbolic at the worst, children really can't always identify with scenarios placed on an exam. To that impoverished student, a breakfast of eggs, toast, and orange juice could be very strange due to her circumstances.

Despite the far-fetched notion of this question, many students cannot relate to the way in which we teach or the way they are asked questions. For instance, so many reading passages and analogies are based on antiquated literature by people who are not like the test takers. Consequently, students are not invested in the tests themselves. The language and the situations do not seem real or accessible. Granted, students should be able to read any passage and answer the questions effectively; however, in giving students passages that turn them off from the desire to test well, we fail our kids. With students being so apathetic or anxious about testing, why not alleviate some of the burdens and struggles that plague their testing?

Apprenticeships

One could take a glance at this title and wonder—what place could apprenticeships possibly have in K12 education? I argue that apprenticeships are a great means to peaking student interest in a career. Subsequently, students will realize how vital various educational skills function in their future endeavors. Apprenticeships will allow for students to have an appreciation for education and the work entailed to be successful in the working arena. While apprenticeships may sound antiquated and outdated, one could think of them as more as personalized internships. While students could also partake in more general internships that are the norm, students could also benefit from the personal attention of a single professional. Partnering our students with mentors in various fields could bring our students to a level of understanding and purpose that they never possessed prior to undertaking an apprenticeship. Just as high schools are moving toward dual-enrollment programs (high school students taking college courses), K12 education needs to adopt students having co-ops—opportunities to work in a field of choice, learn from experts in the field, and gain real world experience of how lessons in the class translate to vocations.

Real World Practicality

As detailed in the previous sections, students need to truly see how school relates to their career interests. Again, I've heard on numerous occasions (especially being an English teacher): "Why do I need to know this?" And in all honestly, sometimes it is next to impossible to try and reason with a child to make them understand the importance of something that they may actually never use again. I believe that everything a child learns is absolutely important, but when students aren't exposed to the real world they cannot understand the importance for themselves. At this point there is truly an issue of compatibility. Education is not compatible with the real world just as the real world is not compatible with education. Rarely do schools have the opportunity to make real world connections with their lessons—and sometimes they do not have the "know-how." Simultaneously however, the real world doesn't make connections to education in meaningful ways. In some regards this harkens back to society and its mindset. How often are scholars glorified—or scientists, researchers, philosophers? As one of my favorite scientists, Neil deGrasse Tyson, expressed, "Why aren't scientists, researchers, philosophers, musicians, and other professions reflected in our Congress?"

We have always been a country focused on upward mobility; however, it has usually been by any means necessary. Unfortunately, personal growth has sometimes been at the demise of other peoples—the systematic genocide of the Native Americans, the slavery of Africans, the exploitation of the Chinese and Irish, among a host of many other atrocities in its history. And now we have reached a point in which personal glamour and appeal outshines productivity and intellect. When entertainment rules a society, it is easy to see how education holds little value. As it stands, a vast majority of our nation's GDP (gross domestic product=the sum of all goods and services) is spent on entertainment and vanity related purchases. It is quite easy to see how little importance education holds within our society.

To add insult to injury, the individuals in these entertainment industries are typically not the poster children of educational attainment. Athletes leave high school and college to enter professional leagues, musicians embark on careers without finishing school, and other entertainers like actors or comedians drop everything to pursue their dreams. While the pursuit of happiness is a noble cause, we tend to deemphasize the true importance of life-long learning and education. Every facet of education and society must work toward having practical connections to one another. Although Americans may chastise Chinese society and culture, there is something to be said for a society that has its students in school twice as long as we do, track students throughout school, and institute family planning that allows for an efficient society. The culture may be hard on students to perform academically, but their success and contribution to the world cannot be understated.

Confines of a Community

I believe that the previous sections illustrate the necessity of diversification within our communities—furthermore, they highlight disparities and disadvantages when comparing different subgroups of society. Ultimately, one has to understand that specific communities only offer specific and potential experiences. As individuals are confined by the things and types of people that inhabit them, they can only grow and learn from those specific aspects. More importantly, our world is becoming all the more globalized. Given that fact, how can our students understand and grow within that context when exposure to other ideas and people are limited? We cannot simply let students read texts by people of different places and ideas—that doesn't create true access. And while technologies that allow us to see satellite images with the click of a keystroke and video chat with people around the world are nice, students need to actually be able to travel. The exposure to different places of the world must be tangible and a priority for students in our schools—especially poorer students that don't have the ability to travel or have varied experiences. Many students today lack the opportunity to travel outside of their immediate communities; and, television is an absolutely unacceptable substitute for personal exposure. Experience, exposure, and travel must be just as essential to classroom instruction if education is to make new leaps and bounds in academic success.

Chapter 7: No Teacher Support

Time

The most valuable resource, to anyone in any field, boils down to the resource of time. Now more than ever, educators are pressed with having significantly less time than needed to properly execute the job. As schools are pressured into having extended school days and extended school years, we significantly limit the amount of time teachers and other educators have to plan and perform. With extended school days and years, a great deal of extra time must be devoted to planning due to more class time, more students, and more assignments to distribute and grade. It is becoming a common occurrence for teachers to receive more students per class and more classes to teach. In extending the school day, no additional time has been provided for teachers to plan for more teaching time and an increased student body. Furthermore, "specials" and/or elective classes (music, art, gym, etc.) are being cut from many school schedules—even recess. Times when teachers would have to plan, tutor, or grade student work are dwindling. It is absolutely appalling that the norm or expected norm is that teachers spend hours in the building after school hours. It is becoming almost necessary for teachers to do so just to manage all of the work asked of them. Additionally, many teachers are expected or required to fulfill other roles outside of teaching—tutoring, coaching, mentoring, leading clubs or groups, as well many other endeavors (some are before or after school responsibilities). To make this scenario more tangible, I'll provide the layout of a schedule that I had.

Staff had to arrive in the building no later than 7:30am—classes began at 8:00am. Usually, up until 8, I would have time to meet with parents or set up my classroom for the day. From 8am to 9am was my "free," or scheduled hour, to plan and grade papers. However, many times I was asked to substitute for a staff member who could not make it to work, to cover for someone who was tardy, attend meetings with staff or parents, or assist with a project that I was not responsible for undertaking; so, most of the time that I had to do a lot of work was not available for me. Following this period, I had a 30 member class of 6th graders from 9am-11am. Lunch was scheduled from 11:00am to 11:30am. After leading my students down to the lunchroom and returning to my classroom, it would be 11:10am. This gave me about 15 minutes to eat lunch. By 11:25am, I needed to be present in the hallways to monitor as students returned from lunch. The next two hours consisted of a 30 member group of 7th graders—followed by another 30 member group of 7th graders. As one could calculate, it would be 3:30pm and time for dismissal. The next 30 minutes would consist of outside duty to watch and monitor students waiting for their rides to pick them up. Staff was allowed to leave and go home at 4pm.

However, with needing to plan upcoming lessons and grade work from the day, I definitely couldn't leave the building at that time. Furthermore, I had students to tutor who didn't understand the lesson's material. I ran a study skills program. I gave piano and voice lessons. I had to be a faculty chair for a school improvement team and be available for staff meetings. Not to mention, teachers cannot be good teachers if they do not continuously learn (and is required by law); therefore, I had to attend my own classes certain days after school and some Saturdays. In working most efficiently, I was able to leave the building at roughly 6pm (sometimes later). With all of those responsibilities, I still needed to drive home and cook and maintain my own home. I've always tried to be health conscious, so I needed to be in bed by 9pm to exercise at 5am the next morning. As one can see, I had no real time to myself. Not trying to create a sob story or elicit sympathy, but teachers should not be worn so ragged. The mental and emotional toll of teaching is draining enough as it is.

It is a matter of health. If a teacher is not healthy and alert, a teacher cannot be effective. If a teacher is not healthy, they will miss work often. If they miss work often, their students will suffer. If their students suffer, then they are a detriment to the learning environment. Absent teachers costs the school money in providing subs (if the school can or even does that). As I mentioned, I ended up subbing quite often. But the most significant point in my opinion boils down to my own personal lifestyle. I was single and had no children. Imagine a father or mother that had that schedule. How could they be attentive to their spouses or children? A work schedule should never put a family's security in jeopardy. Even my own friendships and relationships suffered due to being strained. The weekends simply became a time to quickly see family and friends or take care of responsibilities around the home—and run all of the errands I simply had no time to complete during the week. When one leaves home at 7am and returns home at (or close to) seven, he or she cannot attend to business matters because businesses are closed by that point. Doctors and dentist appointments must be pushed to scheduled school breaks.

And I know what one may think—but, "You have all the time in the world on school breaks!" However, breaks usually become the time when a teacher can catch up on grading and planning and other school responsibilities that got pushed to the backburner during normal weeks. Eastern countries understand that workers need "siestas" (breaks in the schedule or nap times), shorter work days, and more vacation time. They provide better health benefits for their employees. We cannot expect education to improve when we ask educators to do more with fewer resources, less money, and less time! Time is the most precious commodity that educators have—why not maximize it?

Resources

Time is undoubtedly a significant resource, however many other resources are of pertinent value. Many teachers lack essential technologies of the classroom. Many teachers don't have the space, books, instructional materials, or money to do the necessary tasks of educating. In regards to the issue of space, some teachers don't even have their own classrooms—they share with others or use random spaces at random times. And, an overwhelming majority of teachers spend their own money to provide materials for their classes that their schools can't or won't provide. How can our teachers adequately prepare and be ready to instruct their students? But more importantly, how do we move from adequately preparing students to providing instruction at world-class levels all of the time (and everywhere)? Resources can be simply viewed as tools. So, how do we give teachers the tools to make their jobs more streamlined—so they can provide the very best instruction with more time at their disposal? But most importantly, how can we provide more than baseline resources to the students who are most needy?

Aid

In keeping in mind the problem of time and resources, we lose sight of the most underappreciated and underdeveloped resource—people. In thinking of the overwhelming responsibilities that teachers face in the first place, many teachers lose out on having assistance. Truly, one of the greatest collaborative tools for a teacher is to have other adults to assist them. How fair is it for one teacher to be responsible for planning, grading, disciplining, tutoring, teaching, mentoring, and counseling for thirty students or more per class? Teachers are not automatons that can function in isolation without the support of others. Teachers need assistance in the classroom—aid that can help identify students who need more support—or, offer more opportunities to give student feedback on work. Schools need other educators who facilitate the after-school and extracurricular activities that teachers typically manage. Teachers need help from others in planning and grading and having a presence in the classroom.

Unless our governing bodies begin to take class size and teacher expectations seriously, we will not see dramatic positive shifts in educational attainment. Moving forward in this argument, it is impossible to have a school district without having a human resources department. However, humans aren't really treated as resources when we have so few of them. Student to teacher ratios are spiraling out of control. Even when I had a class size of 22, which is manageable, there were so many opportunities for me to have some aid—especially since I had classes of students on many different levels. Teachers should not have to manage students that are on a multitude of grade levels and cognitive abilities—many having diagnosed issues that need the attention of a self-contained (an isolated classroom of particular students with particular difficulties) classroom with a specialist in that issue. It is inconceivable to essentially teach different lessons to groups of students in one class period. Teachers need to be able to focus on delivering one great lesson each day. Teachers should not have to teach multiple grades or multiple subjects. If we truly believed, as a society, in the value of education, then we would allow teachers to have a small group of students and provide them the resources they need to fully instruct at the highest levels.

Extracurricular Pressures and Expectations

In just looking at my own situation on a microcosmic level, I was responsible for undertaking many extracurricular activities. There are literally so many that have happened over time, I cannot even begin to remember them. Beyond late mandatory parent-teacher conferences, I held parent meetings and workshops, led camping or small group student field trips, ran student vs. staff basketball games, talked to reporters on behalf of the school, and a myriad of other activities that I cannot attempt to remember. It is perhaps common sense and common knowledge that the act of multitasking reduces focus on the primary task. When a teacher has to manage all of the aspects of teaching and outside activities simultaneously, it reduces the ability to be most effective at what's the most important—teaching and learning. Given this premise, teaching and learning do not exist in their own isolated cozy bubbles—they are not mutually exclusive. They are mutually inclusive. One cannot have one and not have the other. Educational theorists, researchers, and practitioners refer to the instructional triangle—meaning, true learning occurs when the teacher, the teaching content, and the students are working together as a collaborative unit (and not in pockets or in isolation). If time isn't maximized for the prioritization of these parts of the triangle working together, then we are robbing both teachers and students of the joy of success.

Chapter 8: No Accountability for Parents or Students

Attendance

If there is one "Achilles Heel" to educators, it has to be attendance. I describe it as such because it is one of those variables that an educator has absolutely no control over. The feeling of powerlessness as it pertains to teaching students is an upsetting and debilitating feeling that is difficult to cope with. Attendance, especially in needy districts, is a problem that causes huge disparities in academic success and educational attainment. One may think that the big issue with attendance relates to student absences; however, being tardy is just as disruptive. I have definitely had issues with chronic examples of students missing school. This resulted in students missing the lesson or not receiving the homework to practice the concepts. Beyond that, this clearly happened for each class and subject for that day. When a student misses significant time, they will be unable to perform on quizzes, tests, or exams. It is impossible for a teacher or student to hold one another accountable when one of the parties isn't even present. There is absolutely no reason that a child should miss school unless there is a serious emergency. Unfortunately, this is far from reality when one looks at how attendance plays out in a school environment. Yet, the issue of attendance will be coupled in a chapter to come and expounded upon at that time.

Parent Attitudes

When I think about the attitudes that are held by eastern societies as they relate to teachers, I always feel a little disappointed, sad, and frustrated. Teachers in other countries are held in such high esteem and regarded as professionals. They are leaders of their societies and communities and they are compensated accordingly. However, in America, teachers are not viewed in the same light. Many people regard the teaching profession as something that people practice just to have a job or because they couldn't find anything else to do. People understand that teachers are not compensated well. Given that we live in a very capitalistic society that is founded on the free enterprise system, people tend to have more respect for or regard individuals more highly as their salaries increase. People tend not to respect or regard workers with much admiration when they work in fields that pay little or are within the realm of public service (save firefighting or policing). Anyone that is a janitor, social worker, teacher, or professional of the like are not regarded as important figures in society. In keeping in mind that people includes parents, these mindsets are sometimes harbored by parents that come into schools.

In my opinion, too many parents treat teachers as the enemy when interacting. I've seen on countless occasions parents coming into a school and beginning with confrontation rather than asking questions—or not getting a teacher's side of the story before asking. Essentially, many parents take on the attitude of "what didn't you do?" Parents should really be entering conversations asking their children what they haven't done. Teachers are not the enemy of parents or students. They must be viewed as equal partners and individuals that are there to help their child in any way possible. I've personally experienced this problem on too many occasions. When certain issues arose like grades or class behavior, some parents never spoke to me and went straight to the principals to voice their issue. Unfortunately, they never conversed with me or had the opportunity to sit down with their child and me. Because schools have been put in the position in which keeping students in the school is paramount, parents are beginning to abuse their power. Schools need the funding that comes along for each student; so, parents with multiple students in a school become the ultimate priorities. To upset one of these parents would almost be career suicide. Schools want those parents to be on their good side so they can reap the benefits of the funding from their children. Consequently, parents end up having the knock of "they can do no wrong" in the eyes of the school—"The parent is always right."

Parents are able to come into schools and essentially "raise hell" without consequence. Students are receiving a first-hand example that it is ok to disrespect teachers and educators—but more importantly, that it is ok to disrespect adults in general. Even though one student's parent may not be acting in that manner, the other students are receiving that example from someone else's parent. I have yet to see a consequence issued to a parent or genuine regulations placed on them in regards to how they communicate with teachers and conduct themselves in a building. On a tertiary note, parent conduct transcends communication. I have seen far too many parents come on campuses who are dressed inappropriately, use inappropriate language, use inappropriate substances, and generally interact with their kids or others inappropriately. As was so famously said in the Disney movie *Remember the Titans,* "Attitude reflects leadership." When the leaders of our children (adults) harbor poor attitudes, there is little hope for our students to personify quality attitudes.

Student Attitudes

In being mindful that adult attitudes shape student attitudes, the way in which students conduct themselves is quite disturbing these days. Many students have little respect for adults in the school setting—and that is not to say that it's all of them or all the time. Furthermore, it's not always the most egregious actions; however, small seeds of disrespect blossom into problems that escalate greatly over time. I've had a class that was literally angelic throughout the 1st quarter of the school year. When one student with a very poor attitude, and a popular standing, entered the class during the school year, he absolutely changed the class dynamic. The effect wasn't immediate, but over time the class completely lost its constitution. The negative behavior of the entire class filtered over into their academic performance. As outlined by their beginning of the year diagnostic data, their reading score average was a 44% (obviously very poor). By the end of the first quarter, the class grew significantly to a 77%. Then, following the aftermath of the disruptive student, the scores were abominable and ranged from the 50's and 60's the remainder of the year.

I point this out for a very specific reason. While some would argue that a teacher should have control of his classroom at this point, I fall back to the points outlined in this chapter. The relationship between school, parent, and teacher was flawed. This student was very intelligent and had great test scores (#1). The school wanted to maintain both those test scores and the money the school received for his presence on the roster (#2). Lastly, this student's attitude was reinforced from both the school and his parents (#3). If a school allows a child to be a chronic behavior problem and a continuous problem in every classroom, with every teacher, and with no real consequences (ultimately warranting expulsion), then the other students get the message that negative behavior is acceptable and without serious consequence; therefore, everyone suffered as a result of this one child. Ultimately, again, his behavior was a reflection of adult attitudes. His father was unconcerned about his son's behavior and never called or communicated with teachers about the behavior. Moreover, he issued no consequences at home. Similarly, when addressing the child's behavior from another parent, the mother said, "It's ok, my son is a king."

When the other parent informed her that he was a disruption and a dramatic piece for the girls in the class, that was her response. In this case, the behavior was justified in his eyes and augmented from the flawed behaviors of adults—both the school adults and the parental adults. The old adage holds true—"One bad apple (really can) spoil(s) the bunch." But as my mother used to tell me as a child, "Everyone is the way they are for a reason." In this situation, that message was quite clear. Even if all of the other apples were pure and ripe, something went awry with this spoiled apple. It's not the apple's fault. Some people and some things are definitely responsible. Positive attitudes are just as (if not more) important as positive actions. These mindsets and actions have to be modeled properly for students if they are to possess attitudes that will carry them to future success in all they do.

Student Effort (Intrinsic vs. Extrinsic Motivation)

Perhaps, the notion of student effort could be discussed to the point of exhaustion. In all actuality, it could be tied into adult and student attitudes; but truly, the lack of student effort is a result of many failures from adults—to the form and function of society (a culmination of the factors previously discussed in this book). With the emphases placed on entertainment and vanity in our society, putting forth great effort in school doesn't always seem meaningful to students. Ironically, my colleagues and I have heard students talk about certain lessons or school in general. They would say, "That's not sexy!" Can we really make progress when students are expecting a proverbial light show in regards to what takes place in the learning environment? Teachers are called on, now more than ever, to ensure that their students are engaged and excited about learning. However, it is very hard to compete with the glitz and glamour that our media has to offer. I would argue that it is not wise to even resort to pulling out all of the stops for a child just to learn something.

As a former child and student, I do see the value in making school more enjoyable; but, are we setting students up for success by making them believe that everything has to entertain them? What happens when they enter college—or the work force? As many can attest, there are a plethora of things one has to do in both of those arenas that are remotely fun or exciting. In all actuality, one has to do things they hate or can't stand doing. A significant part of life involves doing things one doesn't want to do in order to reach a point of doing what is desirable. There has to be a sense of struggle and sacrifice to accomplish things in life. The messages that are communicated to children insinuate that if it's not fun than it's not fair. This issue boils down to one major battle—intrinsic vs. extrinsic motivation. As I have observed in and outside of the classroom, students significantly lack intrinsic motivation. Sadly, the times that I have seen students go above and beyond exceeding expectations, they had to be motivated by receiving *something*. People in general cannot expect to accomplish great things if they have to be rewarded for everything. As a society we have essentially grown soft—meaning, we have become a culture of coddling.

Students are now given awards and certificates for merely showing up. While I believe it is great to positively reinforce children, it is totally incompatible with society. In understanding the free enterprise system of capitalism that we function under, the "losers" never receive recognition. So, why do we set up our students to operate in an environment bereft of the values taught in school? Students must understand that the world doesn't work by accomplishing things by always being given something. As cliché as it may sound, our students and children must understand that "hard work pays off." They must truly recognize that hard work is a pay-off in and of itself. As a culture, intrinsic motivation has to be a huge priority in moving our country and our world forward. Ideally, students would come into a learning environment and want to learn. Thus, a teacher would simply have to only worry about teaching. Educational theorists like to say that educators "don't make widgets." (That) Their students are not blank slates that enter a classroom primed to be an intellectual sponge. Students enter classrooms with a whole host of different experiences—positive and negative.

In light of that fact, the problem surfaces as a societal issue writ large. Macrocosmically, we suffer as a culture by not being able to revel in the notion of delayed gratification. Not to harp on clichés again, but we really are a "microwave generation." Technological advances, coupled with the internet and digital media, cultivate a society predicated on instant access. Unfortunately, this phenomenon has handicapped our students by not allowing them to appreciate the work that goes into an accomplishment. As a result, many students are pleased with reading a synopsis instead of an actual book for class. Many students are perfectly content with allowing others to do work for them—as long as they can skate by with a grade—and some students don't even care about their grades. But, truly think about it. As a country and culture, do we advocate for delayed gratification; or, are our televisions flooded with "get rich quick schemes" and regiments that allow one to lose weight "without diet or exercise?" What is our lesson? What is our legacy?

Chapter 9: No Job or Economic Security for Educators

Lack of Competitive Salaries

Point blank, money talks. As alluded to before, most people in society understand and realize that teachers don't earn much money. More disturbing though is the fact that teachers can come into the profession with a wide range of starting salaries—anywhere from the 20ks to the low 40ks. Some schools are attempting to be more competitive with their salaries; however, writ large, teachers are grossly underpaid. One must think about this issue critically; again, we live in a capitalistic society. Quite depressingly, value and worth is quantified by how much one is paid—underpaying expresses a very disturbing message. Additionally, teachers are required (now more than ever) to continuously pursue higher degrees and continuing education.

Given that fact, imagine being a highly qualified and highly educated individual. You have undergone a great deal of schooling and made countless sacrifices; yet, when you are hired, you end up with a salary that forces you to live tightly or pay check-to-pay check. Where is the fairness in that scenario? Typically, a teacher's salary would increase with more advanced degrees in conjunction with additional years on the job. While this structure exists in public schools, many of their budgets are being strained due to decreased funding to public schooling. The state of school pensions is disappearing as a result as well. In terms of schools that do not function by pensions, those who utilize 401ks and personal contribution plans suffer as well (if not more). There are little to no financial incentives for entering the teaching profession. While positions in education on higher levels beyond the classroom exist with competitive salaries, the most important person in education is the teacher. Hands down.

Dwindling Benefits

In conjunction with the issue of competitive salaries, the nature of dwindling benefits in education poses a serious risk to the profession. Again, we have to focus on incentives. People who obtain degrees do so, partly, as a means of establishing a certain lifestyle. Although careers across the board are losing benefits, why would one choose a profession with small salaries and minimal benefits? Especially, consider a teacher with a family. Can they truly provide for their families with small salaries and minimal benefits? At the time, I was single and my benefits were a little more manageable. However, I was also healthier than average at the time as well. My co-pay was 30 dollars for any visit and I had at least a 10 dollar co-pay for my prescriptions. Luckily, I did not have to go to the doctor very often; and, I never had to have any extra procedures outside of cleanings when I went to the dentist.

Considering I had been given an HMO, I couldn't even go to my normal dentist without paying for the majority of just the cleanings. The HMO offered much fewer opportunities for doctors of choice. When I needed a referral to a podiatrist, my HMO doctor referred me.

Upon making the appointment, everything was fine until they said they could not accept me because my HMO hospital affiliation was not compatible with what they accepted. We cannot expect teachers to maintain careers in the profession when so many barriers exist to hinder retaining them. As companies like Google have realized, when you take care of your employees, they become happy, productive, and loyal. With the crisis that is teacher attrition exists, we must do something to ensure that teachers actually remain happy, productive, and loyal.

Evaporating Retirements

When assessing the nature of benefits packages nationally across all careers, the state of retirement packages are degrading. There is something to be said for the legislation that was put forth in the early 20th century in regards to the creation and fortification of unions. At this point, unions are losing power or simply being removed from many corporations—the reality is no different in education. Consequently, there is little protection to ensure employees that they have secured retirements. Essentially, pensions have been replaced by personally funded 401k programs—some employers contribute, but range widely in terms of the percentages. Only a select few people in this country are fortunate enough at this point to receive pensions with their careers. More glaring, however, is the fact that people are finding it more and more unrealistic to have 401ks or the money to contribute enough. People are finding it increasingly impossible to retire at "normal" retirement ages.

Even more troubling is the fact that 401ks are subject to the volatility of our markets—which any investor today could validate its lack of consistency. We are reaching levels of crisis in regards to how people are approaching retirement. Although, in regards to teaching, many teachers are not staying in the profession long enough to benefit from 401k packages or pension plans. The turnover rate in education is so high that schools typically can see a staff attrition of 50% or more. Measures must be taken to solidify legitimate means of staying in the profession and retiring with grace and dignity. It is absolutely disrespectful to educators to call on them to have the most important job in society and cast them to the margins when it comes to securing their economic futures—it's not a money issue. It's an issue of respect and giving educators the means to support themselves and their families.

Disappearing Unions

Although I briefly mentioned the state of unions today, there is a true crisis in regards to its standing in society. Unions were created for the purpose of fair wages, standard job practices, safety, and job benefits. When unions were relevant and prevalent, the middle class was very secure in America. People were able to retire and support their families on one income. Household debt was at a minimum (in the aggregate), and the cases of people going into debt as a result of foreclosures or medical expenses were close to none (in relation to today's market). Unions provide stability, security, and mutual accountability between employers and employees. In spite of the reality that unions are essentially a vestige of a golden age, the level of prestige they had to a workforce remains in other forms. Firstly, again, as salaries increase, the perceived respect usually increases for the employees as well. In a career when teachers are frequently disrespected by society as a whole as well as parents, students, and "superiors," how much incentive exists for a teacher to remain in the profession? In order to preserve the middle class in America, the preservation of the economy, and the security of education, unions must be given the leverage to work symbiotically with districts in order to allow the educational system to thrive.

<u>Chapter 10: The Pain of</u>
<u>Micromanagement</u>

Student Behavior

Any teacher can attest to the level of disarray that can overtake a classroom due to student behavior. I would be a rich man if I had a dollar for every time someone said, "Oh, I'm sorry," or "I feel bad for you" when I told them I was a teacher. I would hear sentiments like, "I couldn't deal with kids these days. They are so bad and they don't listen." Negative student behavior is the biggest hindrance to student success and teacher sanity within a classroom. Poor student behavior can become the main focus in the classroom, for administrators, and for students alike. It can detract so much from a classroom that it makes teachers discouraged about their jobs—not that they don't care about the students, but going into a disruptive environment is hardly tempting. The average person fails to account for and fully think about the consequences of one (or a group) student(s) with poor behavior. Students who are disruptive prevent others from learning. They take attention away from lessons and place it on behavior and buffoonery. Additionally, there are usually a handful of students who egg on the behavior and/or are active participants but not the catalysts. On the other hand, there are other students who are passive and affirm the behavior through laughter or other means. Lastly, there are those students who sit off to the side and do not speak out against negative behavior. Each type of student is responsible and accountable for the actions of the classroom. Just as "unpopular" students are ostracized for being "un-cool," disruptive students are rarely, if never, made pariahs for their behavior.

As one could surmise, rarely do students speak out against such behaviors in any strong force to eliminate negative behaviors in the classroom. Consequently, these mindsets have led to creating environments that allow bullying to thrive. It seems almost impossible to turn on a news report these days and not see a program special on bullying and its effects in today's classrooms. Districts and states are even putting legislation on the books to counter the results of bullying. The nature of bullying has created an epidemic in which students are suffering from serious emotional and physical ramifications—some students have even lost their lives as a result of "hazing" or suicide. The compounding of these issues takes a toll on the learning environment and the safety of schools. Police presence and/or added security have even been a necessity on some school campuses. Hence, we cannot legitimately expect students or teachers to stay in school environments in which student behavior becomes a mitigating force in regards to a healthy school culture, safety, or academic success.

Student Engagement

The notion of student engagement is a responsibility that is placed upon teachers regularly. It is true that teachers should create lessons that are engaging for students; however, at some point, students must build up some kind of mental fortitude. The tasks that will be necessary at the next level of education or career will entail things that are not "fun." We cannot pamper and coddle our students in a way that won't build up their sense of personal responsibility to engage in their own learning. As great adult learners know, one must find something intriguing about what one has to learn in order to make the learning meaningful and retained. Contemporarily, students tend to possess an attitude that is anti-learning or anti-school. When one embodies a mindset that counters the culture of learning, allowing one to engage one's self in learning becomes difficult at the least. In harkening back to the notion of negative student attitudes, the process of engagement becomes strained when one initially has a negative attitude. As a society, we must take on the task of encouraging students to want to be successful in school—that C's are not acceptable—that mediocre will not cut it. Being engaged in school must become just as "sexy" as the thrill that athletic competition presents in society. Students, parents, teachers, and communities at large must work collaboratively to inspire and motivate students to want to be engaged in their own learning.

Student Morality

Attitudes, mindsets, and behaviors have a concise and direct correlation amid one another. I tend to think of morals as almost being a value structure that is rooted in spirituality or religious belief; however, morality goes beyond attitudes and basic mindsets. It is a compass that guides and formulates attitudes and mindsets. So essentially, it is the foundation of future behaviors. Students all too frequently get caught up in cliques, gangs, bullying, cheating, plagiarism, as well as a wide array of other behaviors that detract from the learning environment.

Ironically, this whole issue reminds me of elders who say, "We lost education when we took religion out of schools." I am not advocating that we should have religion in schools at all—what I do advocate for is religious acceptance as well as a full-hearted belief in the separation of church and state. On the other hand, students do suffer by not receiving a form of morality being emphasized or taught in the school.

The proliferation of violence, bullying, and apathy in schools is a plague and a crisis within our schools. The use of counselors, deans, truancy officers, policemen and women, and social workers has overrun many of our schools. Schools are continuously calling on the support of third parties to provide services to their students as a means of maintaining safe environments that are conducive for learning. If educators have to deal with the lack of student morality, then poor behavior and academic inferiority will take precedence over actually educating. In my experience, and those of many of my colleagues, mentors, and former colleagues, instructors spend the same, if not more, time disciplining than they do in instruction—this cannot be the norm if we are to reach a level of great educational attainment in this country.

Intangibles

It may be difficult to reason having a section that focuses on the qualities of a student that are not directly taught; however, society is failing to develop students that are well-rounded—holistic education is an aspect of schools that gets lost in the shuffle. Too many students are forced to simply be students, or athletes, or dancers, or musicians, or whatever pressures are placed upon them. Furthermore, schools are creating systems that limit the ability for students to be well-rounded.

Study hall times are being eliminated along with activities like recess. Arts programs are being cut in schools. Consequently, how can our students be well-rounded and obtain intangible skills that can augment their learning and function in society? In walking into any school, one could easily see the range of types of students and their interests and quirks. Looking at the range of students reminds me of a former student of mine. She could hardly sit still and frequently got in trouble for skipping, running, or dancing. The school structure was an extended day—classes went from 8am-5pm. Throughout the whole course of this day, students did not have one period other than lunch in which they were not engaged in some type of instruction. She simply wanted to dance.

After a colleague enrolled her into a dance studio outside of school, she began to flourish and be motivated when she was engrossed in her studies. On many occasions, students simply need an arena in which they can express themselves and explore their interests. However, when we limit possibilities for students to expand themselves, we limit the potential they have to discover what is most important of all—themselves. So, when can students develop themselves holistically when constrained under the confines of modern schools? Although students may never formally utilize some opportunities like the arts, study halls, and group gathering times, these programs develop students socially, emotionally, and intellectually. Students must have opportunities to explore their other interests to become well-rounded citizens. Most successful adults do not function as strict automatons—they rely on outside interests and interpersonal skills that facilitate meaningful experiences in their adult lives.

Chapter 11: Digital Dummies

A Language Lost

As a former English teacher, this aspect of poor educational attainment troubles me immensely. The inundation of technology into the lives of our children has wreaked havoc on their ability to perform in the classroom. As linguists have noticed for many years now, countercultures, vernacular, and different colloquialisms have made it difficult for people to properly grasp English. It is quite straightforward that Standard English dominates the world of academia and business. Our students are attempting to navigate those fields and they lack the proper foundation in its structure. More devastating however is the fact that students are making it all the more impossible for themselves in terms of grasping the language well enough. In our world of abbreviations, acronyms, emoticons, and text message language, students are not developing and/or forget the standard methods of reading and writing. While our youth are quite inventive in their innovative ways of communication, it is killing the adolescent mind's development and true potential.

In having to grade student writing frequently, I encountered the use of text lingo, abbreviations, and just overall colloquialisms from even the strongest students—students that excelled on virtually every standardized test one could imagine. Unfortunately, when those students have to produce college writing, they will be overwhelmingly ill-equipped. It is no wonder or secret as to why so many colleges and universities are complaining about the need to enroll more "college-ready" students. These institutions are being forced to remediate students just to have them at a ground level for being able to take on the rigors of collegiate work. Students are missing out on the experience of engaging with language at a higher level that challenges on a personally emotional and cognitive level.

Not to say that I am a language purist, but there is something to be said about having a language disemboweled and turned on its head. All languages undergo change and transformation; however, students cannot continue to speak and write one way when they will have to communicate entirely differently in the professional world. There can only be two options that remain: either kids will grow up entirely being engrossed in Standard English at school, in the home, or their communities; or, we will have to totally block the use of variations of English. Considering the latter is totally impossible, as a society, we must make it a top priority to expose kids to a broad range of vocabulary in the context of Standard English. When students have a mastery over the language, they will be primed and poised to take on the academic rigors of school. And better yet, they will be able to expand and use vernacular and colloquialisms properly to express themselves—in the right time and place. It is just like I tell my English or music students—once you learn the rules, then you can learn when and how to break them.

Human Interaction

As a consequence of our over indulgence in technology, students are shifting social norms in very strange ways. In comparison to previous generations that focused on interpersonal skills and direct communication, students today heavily rely on text messaging, chatting, and emailing. The lack of human interaction poses great risks not only to our students, but to society as a whole as well. The psychological and emotional development of students is lost in the proverbial shuffle when they have few opportunities to read vocal inflection, body language, and facial expressions. As our world becomes ever more focused on personal interactions in the corporate world, how can our students be prepared for that environment when they lack genuine social experiences?

Not to be taboo, but even a sense of human touch is important in cultivating strong human interactions. Although, I'm not saying that people need to be going around touching one another. What I am advocating for is the necessity to understand subtle forms of touching that naturally occur in conversation. Many students frequently complain about not being able to work in groups or "get along" with others for a multitude of reasons. The lack of quality and meaningful human interaction is preventing our students from functioning well in schools and developing properly in regards to their psychological and emotional standing. Face-to-face human interaction, without augmentation or supplementation, must be prioritized in schooling when students are communicating.

Plugged In

Although the idea of being "plugged in" refers to many Americans, being inundated in technology is a huge issue among students today. MIT has even noticed an issue with its undergraduate students multitasking and being sidetracked with technology. If a prestigious *higher education* institution is plagued by this phenomenon, what hope do we have for public education writ large? Students are constantly being tied into Facebook, Twitter, Instagram, as well as a barrage of other online platforms. Unfortunately, students bring these online identities and issues into the classroom on a daily basis. More importantly, students attempt to use them throughout the school day and rather frequently when they are at home. Instructional and homework time are strained and misused because many students are engrossed in the distracting medium that is computer technology. It is very difficult for many students to not want to "live" in the digital world. The pull on students to constantly be in an alternative world is tempting to say the least.

The proliferation of online avatars has given people the means to "escape" the real world. Unfortunately, students remain passively or actively engaged in the digital world even when he or she is not presently using technology. Many students express their inability to function without checking their technological devices frequently—even using them during homework or other important activities. Despite the hyperbolic nature of current technologically related personal issues, scientists are expressing the notion that humans are essentially becoming cybernetic. We are so interconnected with technology that it is becoming an extension of ourselves. While this is very helpful in situations when individuals need prosthetics or life-saving technologies, the reliance on digital media for everyday experiences provides a false sense of reality. Students must be grounded in reality if they are to remain focused on their studies and academic excellence.

Entertain Me So I Can Be Lazy

A former colleague of mine once told me that kids today are the "Make Me" generation. His rationale was that students embody the idea of "I can learn, but can you make me?" As previously discussed, students frequently make comments about how school isn't fun or enjoyable—that they need to be entertained and engaged in ways that mimic video games or other all-immersive mediums. School is not one of those mediums! Many teachers can attest to the nature of students and their insistence on being bored—even when an engaging activity is taking place in the classroom. Ironically, these sentiments even surface during gym and field trips—activities that were the highlight of school days for my peers and me when I was a student. In keeping in mind the societal trends surrounding entertainment, our economy is driven greatly by products and services that provide entertainment.

Unfortunately, these sentiments trickle down into the happenings of the day-to-day events in classrooms and schools. The level of educational dullness and apathy amongst our students is proving to be a detrimental detraction in regards to academic success. Students must understand that school is not a vehicle for providing entertainment—instructionally or socially. It needs to be understood and respected as a regal environment that is a learning institution. When educators gripe about the levels of immaturity that imbrue all levels of education, they are expressing the disillusionment that stems from students not working hard. I would argue, in the aggregate, students today are very lazy. The image and paradigm of the lethargic student must be removed from the veracity of schools today. Yes, technologies and advances in society are making it easier for humans to do less and achieve more. But, the same cannot be true for education. Students must understand and buy-in (with the support of all adults in society) to the notion that education is about doing more to reach even greater heights.

Chapter 12: Different Schools for Different Folks

Personality

One of, if not, the most important topics in education today revolves around differentiated instruction. The educational world is working toward meeting the learning needs of all different types of students—whether they learn best visually, aurally, tactilely, or kinesthetically. However, education is not moving toward the next level of differentiation. Corporations and sports teams subscribe to differentiation themselves. How many times have *you* noticed organizations ensuring they have the right mix of personalities on their teams? These industries realize the importance of harmony amongst people to ensure strong cultural environments. Considering these various organizations value the need for all parties being on one accord, why isn't the same practice modeled in education? Shouldn't the personalities of students in a classroom mesh well? Shouldn't the personality of a teacher mesh well with the students? Given the advances in psychological research, many tests and gauges have been put in place to assess the personality types of people.

I argue that students need to take simple personality types at the beginning of school years and semesters. Students are given a whole host of other diagnostic tests at the beginning of semesters of education. Why can't the same be replicated for assessing personalities? Imagine a classroom that functioned seamlessly just because someone took the time to ensure that students function as a whole—and better yet, when involved in small groups. While personality tests do not define one perfectly, they provide great insight into how groups of people will most likely function and interact together. Due to the fact that many students struggle with "getting along" with others, especially in small groups, the level of focus and academic achievement could ascend to new heights with the implementation of personality tests. Class rosters could be constructed based on personality tests to provide further security in regards to the harmony of a class environment. When so many schools and classes struggle with levels of discord or poor culture, why not make the small investment up front to improve classroom culture—and most importantly, student achievement?!

Learning Styles

Similar to the necessity of ensuring class compatibility as it relates to personality, schools and classes need to formulate class rosters based on student learning styles as well. Coupling the power of personality compatibility and learning style needs would revolutionize every classroom environment. Instead of trying to make teachers instruct to many different types of learners, allow them to focus on delivering a great lesson based more on one rather than several. Students that learn best in the same fashion, collected in one class, would learn at the highest level possible. They would feel comfortable being around the same type of learners and more open to learning from their peers. If our society is sincerely attempting to become serious about education, then we will invest in providing more resources to schools. Districts must be empowered to hire the staff to instruct classrooms that have varied personality and learning styles. Too often in education, everything comes down to money. However, everything in life is not about money—although society seems to focus on it far too often. Money cannot be an object when the state of our future is at stake. The educational attainment of our students today solidifies or destroys future possibilities. As the song says, "The children are our future . . ." As cheesy and cliché as it is, students truly are the future. In order to ensure the security of our world at large, we cannot fail to provide every opportunity to teach at the highest levels possible. Our students deserve it. We deserve it. And our future depends on it.

Specialty Schools

In understanding that students actually do come to the table with a diverse body of experiences, talents, and skills, schools need to cater to those special attributes. Essentially, more music, culinary, dance, technical, etc. schools need to exist to give students options for their education. Students need to feel that the content that they learn every day is applicable and relevant to their interests and future pursuits. Although students may not go into those specialties in the future, the buy-in that students would have into their educations would be priceless. Students would want to go to school, work hard, and invest in their learning. Now, this entails that as a society we invest heavily in education. Schools would still need to utilize devices like personality and learning style tests to cater to specific needs within the classroom;

however, we must take the next step and differentiate between types of schools. Students and parents need choice in the types of schools they attend. Simultaneously, these students need schools that still cater to their individual personalities and learning needs. At some point, schools must move away from being in competition with one another. In creating streamlined databases between schools, student data and information would be able to be easily shared and utilized between districts and even states.

Most people witnessed the debacle that ensued from 9-11 when the CIA and FBI failed to share information effectively. The same problems arise when schools and districts cannot do the same. If schools were able to securely link databases, then a school that noticed a child may benefit more from being in a different specialty school could direct them to the appropriate channels. But, as long as schools are overly focused on retaining their own students for the purpose of maintaining their funding, then we'll never actually start doing what is best for kids—that is the whole point of educating or working in education. Additionally, distance, transportation, or residency couldn't be an issue. If there is a specialty school that would work best for a student from a different county or district, that student should still be able to attend with no penalty or cost. Perhaps I may be painting a picture of some blissful paradisiacal oasis, but this is how things need to be. If we truly love our children and care about our future, then this must happen.

Alternative Schools

I hate to be the bearer of bad news, but alternative schools have to exist as well. Not to demonize kids, but those who cannot or refuse to function within the confines of school rules need an alternative form of schooling. These schools can have better resources in terms of counselors and social workers. Furthermore, these schools would have more fortification in terms of deans, security, and mentorship. I hate to propose school buildings that are so structured and focused on behavior, but students who have exhausted all other forms of intervention need a specialty school of their own. It is disturbing how many of our youth end up in juvenile detention centers, boot camps, and other reactionary behavior systems. The strain that corrections put on our system is unacceptable. We lose so many of our students to, mostly, petty crimes and extenuating circumstances. The number of youth being incarcerated has risen greatly—even amongst kids that are not legally adults. So many prisons are being privatized and subsidized by various groups—even our governments. Doesn't it seem problematic that multi-million dollar prisons are being built when so many of our schools are being closed? What message is being sent to society in regards to our priorities? There is a dollar-for-dollar correlation between educational expenditures and corrections. Investing more in education limits the number of offenders that will wind up in the justice system.

In my hometown of Detroit, schools receive around $7000 per student. In contrast, the total cost to house an inmate for one year is about $30,000 dollars. I don't know about you, but I would much rather have $30,000 of my tax dollars to go to educating children and $7000 go towards inmates. Imagine how different student outcomes would be if we displayed genuine interest in their learning by investing accordingly—as the American motto goes, "Money talks." In our capitalistic economy, value is derived by the amount of money that is spent or invested in something. In providing schooling for these struggling students, we could provide the rehabilitation that they actually require. There is no better rehabilitation than receiving an education and having the tools necessary to make a better life for one's self. The differentiation of schools themselves must then occur—and we must make room for alternative schools. Our personal, physical, economic, and mental security relies on reducing crime and increasing the number of productive citizens we have in our world.

Chapter 13: Parenting (The Coup de Grâce)

No Value for Education (Expectations)

Not that a lot of parents don't realize the importance of education, but not enough parents address educational expectations properly. In simplest terms, many parents are not doing what is necessary to ensure that their children succeed. The lack of parenting is the one true reason why children do not succeed today. I have outlined several factors over the course of this book that link directly to parent actions—the nuclear family, attendance, lack of exposure, and parent attitudes/mindsets. One of the first factors that I discussed was the lack of vocabulary to which a child is exposed. Again, the number one indicator of child success in education is the amount of vocabulary that he or she enters school with—in pre-school or kindergarten. Consequently, this language acquisition comes about before children are in school. This is the responsibility of parents and adults that raise those children—what they do and do not say around them. Babies and toddlers must be spoken to frequently and with a broad array of words and phrasings. Early childhood psychologists and researchers note that doing "baby talk" to small children is detrimental to their ability to understand the normal structures of language and speech because it varies from the way adults communicate. Furthermore, it impedes on their language acquisition and their ability to retain words and their meanings. This lack of parenting handicaps a child for their rest of their lives—and it begins before they even step foot in a school.

Ironically, it seems that so many parents have the expectation that schools are solely responsible for the wellbeing of their child. When one takes on this mindset, they totally miss the true value and purpose of education. Parents and society have unrealistic expectations for what schools are meant to do. Some schools now provide three meals a day, nurses, social workers, counselors, officers, special educators, latchkey, tutoring, transportation, etc . . . the list goes on and on. Schools cannot provide everything a child needs. What other industry is responsible for producing one goal but held accountable to a multitude of outside factors that are beyond their control? Why do parents and our communities expect schools to be the end-all of student achievement? Parents must place a value on education that exceeds everything else for a child. With that being addressed, the following sections will elaborate on how many parents fail to truly value education.

Uneducated Adults

As mentioned previously, half of the adult population in this country are functionally literate. What message is being sent to children in regards to the value of education when their parents and adults around them aren't adequately educated? Furthermore, if our adults aren't educated, how can they help children navigate through the world of education to achieve? At this point in our history, we have one ugly cycle of a lack of education being played out in communities and families. When one analyzes the nature of race and class in our society, those populations in the minority are the ultimate victims of this cycle. Poverty is a direct indicator of a lack of educational attainment; and, speaking English as a foreign language is a direct indicator of a difficulty in educational success in this country as well. Considering minority populations are growing ever so sharply and overtaking the majority, this perverse cycle culminates as a civil rights issue. In order to improve our country, adult education must become an important priority. Interestingly enough, the type of education that needs to take place for adults must go far beyond just subject matters. A great deal of adults need family planning as well as parenting classes to be ready to raise their children—an adult population that must understand the value of education—a population ready to be able to make education the supreme priority in the home by ensuring their children's success by any means necessary.

No Involvement

If anything illustrates a lack of parental value for education, the lack of involvement does for sure. Poor parental involvement is a reality of many different faults. Does a parent read to their children all of the time—especially as babies, toddlers, and young children? Frequently reading to and with a child develops their language abilities and their love of reading and learning—skills and mindsets that are essential to educational success. Does a parent attend all parent teacher conferences and volunteer for activities at the school? Being active in the school life of a child communicates its importance through the parental support. Does a parent know their child's teachers and communicate with them often? Does a parent work with their children every evening and help with homework? These are just but a few of the things that absolutely set a child in their ability to be successful in school. With that in mind, there are a myriad of campaigns that call for adults to be active in school, to build mentorship, and to adopt. It is proven that adult involvement in a child's life and endeavors exponentially enhance a child's ability to learn. Most success for a child starts in the home—from having active and supportive parents that model what educational excellence looks like.

Unfortunately, these scenarios play out far too often when it comes to my experiences, those accounted, and those my colleagues have had. In light of that, parent/teacher conferences have been a clear indicator of child success. I cannot recall the number of times my colleagues have expressed that the parents who come to conferences are not the parents that need to be seen in the first place. It is the parents that do not show up whose kids are typically struggling and need the extra attention and support of their parents. However, parent/teacher conferences are only a small part of what becomes important in terms of parental involvement. I communicate with dozens upon dozens of teachers regularly and they share similar sentiments. Many schools and teachers try to come up with programs or incentives to just get parents in the door. Should schools really have to try and manipulate parents to be involved with *their* children; or, should parents just be doing it on their own? Clearly, the correct choice would be the latter.

Although, some parents do partake in various forms of involvement; however, sometimes the forms of involvement are inappropriate or not coupled with things that are of more significance—for example: many parents will be very involved with their students when it comes to extracurricular activities. I've seen parents, who never show up to parent conferences or communicate about academic affairs to educators, attend every sports event or program in which their child is involved. It is absolutely wonderful to support one's children in their extracurricular activities. But, when a parent doesn't make a child perform well in school first before taking part in these activities, the wrong message is sent. Parental involvement is not just action—it is a mindset. Parents must be partners with teachers and their children to work with them in building a child. As a proud educator, I honestly become infuriated when I hear some of the stories from my students or their parents. I have students who literally go home and do nothing but watch T.V. and play video games, or surf the web, or talk on the phone—these students have noted that in some cases they don't interact with their parents or even have dinner with them.

The breakdown of our familial structures has decimated the ability for children to succeed today. On a tertiary note, one of the most frustrating moments of my career was when a student came to school and couldn't stay awake. He informed me that his mom was out partying and he was dropped off at his aunt's house. His mom finally picked him up after 2am and he had to wake up around 5am to get to school. The gross negligence that takes place in many homes is a force that is almost impossible to combat for educators—many parental behaviors are utterly untenable. While this may seem an extreme case, so many other scenarios that I have observed are actually far worse. I figured that providing a rather "in-between" example would be more suitable and more jarring. Ultimately, parents have to be constantly active in their child's life in regards to their education—and not just when they get to school, but from the moment they enter the world.

Child Priorities

One of the most direct and honest statements that I can express may be controversial at the least—parents should not and cannot have children when they are not ready. Granted, people make mistakes and things happen. That goes without question. But on the whole, family planning has to be a point of emphasis for the health of our families. If parents cannot be committed and ready to do *everything* in their power to raise their children and be involved in their children's lives, then they have no business having or raising children. It is sad and simultaneously astonishing how many kids are currently born to single parents, raised by people other than their mother or father, in foster care, homeless, or a drop in the bucket compared to how many siblings they have—many with siblings from different mothers and/or fathers and (a disproportionate number) products of low-income or poverty-stricken homes. Whereas many guardians fail in directing their child's priorities, guardians fail in making that child *their* priority. Too many children do not understand the value of earning things. As I have observed across various types of schools in equally variant communities, many children receive contradictory and conflicting messages. The occurrences are simply enumerable as they relate to conflicting messages to children.

For example, many students receive luxuries like the latest in trendy fashions, phones, video games, iPads and iPods, as well as many other luxury items; yet, the students are disruptive in school, receive poor grades, or even act out disrespectfully towards adults—even to their own parents or guardians. Bluntly, students cannot be given these items unless they are earned. Unless a child is behaving wonderfully, doing well in school, and taking care of their business, they shouldn't have these things or be going out to enjoyable places. What message does it send to a child that is doing poorly in school and can still hang out with friends on the weekends, receive their favorite things, and still act out? Unfortunately, the lack of consequences and preventative measures appear to be synonymous to those seen in education as well. Nevertheless, schools cannot effectively enforce discipline measures when they are not being reciprocated at home. Unless there is a clear bridge between the two, public education will continue to be abysmal as compared to our counterparts globally. Parents are failing our kids; thus, our children fail to fully achieve when they enter their respective school buildings.

Chapter 14: The Lost Generation of Teachers and Students

Teaching Talent

Teaching talent is becoming a lost art. One has to first keep in mind all of the factors that are making teaching a relic of the past. First, teachers are made to teach to large class sizes with a student population that ranges in grade level as well as cognitive abilities—classrooms are blended between general education students and special education students—not to mention the variation in student personalities and learning styles. When one couples these issues with budget cuts and the proliferation of charter schools, a recipe for disaster is created. Essentially, teachers are being paid less with fewer benefits and asked to do more. In making this example come to life a little more, I'll reuse my NFL analogy. What happens when a superstar player feels slighted by his team? He packs his bags and goes to a team that will pay him and show him respect. Now imagine, every superstar did this at the same time. But, they found out they could receive more benefits if they left playing football all together. This is what has become of education today. Many of the teachers that are good at their jobs and like teaching simply cannot stay in the profession because they end up struggling so much in their own personal lives.

Consequently, a large pool of teachers end up being young and inexperienced; furthermore, they are put into an educational arena that now fails to support teachers because they provide so little yet demand so much. Sadly, districts are even incentivizing veteran teachers to retire or leave the profession. In doing so, the district can spend less money by paying young teachers fewer dollars; and, they can exercise more control over those newer teachers because they are inexperienced, naïve, and/or just happy to have a job. Despite the great number of young teachers that exist out there, at the end of the day, they are suffering and are not being provided the resources to teach most effectively. Therefore, if only the ills that were outlined in the previous chapters could be addressed, then the loss of teaching talent would not be an issue.

As most educational research says, the teacher can make all of the difference. Given the previously outlined problems in regards to the treatment of teachers, so many educators become frustrated and jaded. The turnover rate of teachers is overwhelmingly high. Most recent research suggests that teachers only stay within the profession from 2-5 years at this point. What type of expertise is generated in that time—especially when a teacher is stressed and under-resourced? As a result, an ugly pattern emerges. Schools expect teachers to burn out quickly; however, they tend to be perfectly content with that paradigm. They get a couple of years from teachers at a low cost; then, they'll just hire the next batch of young teachers and do the same thing all over again. Hence, the ugly head of "Capitalism on Steroids" rears its ugly head once more. Schools cut the overhead, and they profit . . .

Teacher Retention

Based on the text from the previous section, it is quite apparent that retaining teachers becomes a major issue. And yes, the lack of teacher retention diminishes the quality of teachers that exist do to a lack of experience and meaningful professional development. Yet, there is another glaring problem that arises as a result that is tantamount—perhaps paramount. Tangentially, we lost sight of the character and holistic development of students. This relates as it pertains to student sentiments on developing long healthy relationships. When I was in school, teachers taught in a building for their careers. Each year, I could bank on which teacher I would have. When I was growing up, my sister was six grade levels ahead of me; yet, I knew in six years, I would have the same teachers. A level of healthy expectations, relationships, and culture building was able to naturally occur due to the strength of teacher retention. But, why is this important? The true importance presents itself more starkly in our more disadvantaged communities.

Students that experience a level of high turnover with teachers undergo some serious psychological and emotional scars. They are made to feel that people don't truly care about them and/or will only stick with them for a short while. It is somewhat reminiscent and analogous to those sitcoms that illustrate the scenario of parents getting a divorce and trying to communicate the experience to their child. Many children in this situation end up feeling that they are somehow at fault—that they are the problem. Most depressingly, students suffer through these experiences every year at many schools—many having a 50% turnover rate or higher. To make the point more clearly, my students were very direct in expressing these sentiments. However, they did not reveal these feelings until the end of the school year. They expressed, "Yeah, we tried to get you fired in the beginning Mr. James." By the time they realized I wouldn't go anywhere, they let up. The true message that is being communicated here is that students are expecting to be let down; so, to prevent that pain, they try to control their own situations (by trying to get me fired and make life harder on me unfortunately). But, I came to find out that they had three English teachers quit in the middle of the year the year before I taught them. Teacher retention is so much more than dollars and cents. It's more than just having great teachers. It is about having committed adults to be continuous positive forces in the lives of children.

The Frozen Fire

Perhaps this is the poetic side of me surfacing, but the intensity of classrooms reminds me of a frozen fire—a metaphor for the dullness children have in regards to their educations. Once more, I think back to one of my favorite scientists, people, and social commentators (Neil deGrasse Tyson). He frequently admonishes our government for cutting funding to NASA and other scientific or space-faring related endeavors. He recalls the 50s and 60s when the American public was enthralled with the competition with the Russians in exploring the skies. The picture he paints of an inspired public reveals the pioneering fervor that led to many of our world's greatest innovations. The period that spanned from the 50s to the 70s was a time of awe and wonder at what could be done and created in the world. Education was different; and, society (and more importantly, parents) reflected the importance of it. Support and involvement illustrated a much different picture.

Moreover, when our current media pushes "Reality" T.V. and programs that contain no educational or cultural value, it is no surprise that we have children who lack any passion towards learning. That era donned *Star Trek, Star Wars,* and historic NASA Apollo missions. These cultural phenomenons inspired a generation and spawned an era of innovation that paved the way for the space shuttle and the internet. This generation had something to make them dream. What do kids today have to truly dream about? Being a professional athlete? A dancer? A singer? These professions are not rooted in educational attainment nor does society urge its necessity in these pursuits. What hope do we have as a culture, a society, and a world when we fail to inspire our children to aim high and achieve more?

Apathy

Who cares?

This question truly sends fear through my entire body when I think of the answer to this question. I recoil at the very thought of the true answer—apparently, it seems like very few, if no one. You may be thinking—I care! And, perhaps you do. But, when one truly cares, they do something. When I think about how apathetic society is becoming, I tend to doubt the ability for education to improve. One of the most profound lines that I have ever heard was stated in a rather unassuming movie—*The Boondock Saints.* A priest in the movie professed, "Now, we must all fear evil men. But there is another kind of evil which we must fear most, and that is the indifference of good men." If those who can make change do not, then we will forever be stuck in the same place—over and over and over again.

In analyzing the previous generations of the 50s, 60s, and 70s, there is a clear difference in what people will actually do now. People held rallies. People marched. People stared down the barrel of guns and risked imprisonment. People braved dogs being released on them and the threat of lynching and bombing. Some were referred to as rioters, rebels, freedom fighters, or even terrorists or criminals. But, there is something to be said for those individuals that made a difference and changed our world for the better. What are we doing now? Personally, I am contributing in the best way that I am equipped and know how. I am writing this very text. I just wonder when words will turn to revolution. We cannot continue on this path of failure and mediocrity. We cannot continue to have the masses not care or not do anything to change this reality. Our government frequently attempts to initiate measures to improve education. Perhaps they care; but, do they? Our federal government imparted the power of education to the states. Ultimately, the federal government dumped that responsibility on each individual state. Well, I guess they don't fully care enough either. Who are we left with, and when will *they* win?

References

Altbach, P., Berdahl, R., & Gumport, P. (2005). *American Higher Education in the Twenty-First Century.* Baltimore: Johns Hopkins University Press.

Anyon, J. (1997). *Ghetto Schooling: A Political Economy of Urban Educational Reform.* New York: Teachers College Press.

Baker, B. D., Libby, K., Wiley, K., & University of Colorado at Boulder, N. (2012). Spending by the Major Charter Management Organizations: Comparing Charter School and Local Public District Financial Resources in New York, Ohio, and Texas. *National Education Policy Center.*

Bartkus, V., & Davis, J. H. (2009). *Social Capital : Reaching Out, Reaching In / Edited by Viva Ona Bartkus and James H. Davis.* Cheltenham, UK; Northampton, MA: Edward Elgar, c2009.

Benner, G. J., Nelson, J., Sanders, E. A., & Ralston, N. C. (2012). Behavior Intervention for Students with Externalizing Behavior Problems: Primary-Level Standard Protocol. *Exceptional Children, 78*(2), 181-198.

Billett, P. (2012). Lessons From the Field: Ethics in Youth Social Capital Research. *Youth Studies Australia, 31*(3), 43.

Bolman, L., & Deal, T. (2008). *Reframing Organizations: Artistry, Choice, and Leadership.* San Francisco: Jossey-Bass.

Bottles, K. (2012). Reverse Innovation and American Health Care in a Time of Cost Crisis. *Physician Executive, 38*(4), 18-20.

Brewer, D. J., & McEwan, P. J. (2010). *Economics of Education [electronic resource]*. Burlington : Elsevier Science, 2010.

Carpenter-Aeby, T., & Aeby, V. (2012). Reflections of Client Satisfaction: Reframing Family Perceptions of Mandatory Alternative School Assignment. *Journal Of Instructional Psychology*, *39*(1), 3-11.

City, E., Elmore, R., Fiarman, S., & Teitel, L. (2009). *Instructional Rounds in Education*. Cambridge: Harvard Education Press.

Cook, K., & Loomis, C. (2012). The Impact of Choice and Control on Women's Childbirth Experiences. *Journal Of Perinatal Education*, *21*(3), 158-168. doi:10.1891/1058-1243.21.3.158.

Conley, B. (2002). *Alternative Schools: A Reference Handbook / Brenda Edgerton Conley*. Santa Barbara, Calif. : ABC-CLIO, c2002.

Costley, K. C., & Harrington, K. (2012). Character Education: A Growing Need in American Schools. *Online Submission*.

Damme, D. V., Karkkainen, K., & Organisation for Economic Cooperation and, D. (2011). OECD Education Today Crisis Survey 2010: The Impact of the Economic Recession and Fiscal Crisis on Education in OECD Countries. OECD Education Working Papers, No. 56. *OECD Publishing*.

David A., S., & Thomas M., S. (n.d). Explaining the Gap in Charter and Traditional Public School Teacher Turnover Rates. *Economics Of Education Review*, *31*(Special Issue: Charter Schools), 268-279. doi:10.1016/j.econedurev.2011.09.007.

Draxton, S., Radley, K., Murphy, J., Nevin, A., Nishimura, T., Hagge, D., & Taniform, L. (2011). *Challenging the Achievement Gap by Disrupting Concepts of "Normalcy." The Complete Essays*. Online Submission.

Duderstadt, J., & Womack, F. (2003). *The Future of the Pubic University in America: Beyond the Crossroads*. Baltimore: 2003.

Galunic, C., Ertug, G., & Gargiulo, M. (2012). The Positive Externalities of Social Capital: Benefiting From Senior Brokers. *Academy Of Management Journal, 55*(5), 1213-1231.

Gerstel, N. (2011). Rethinking Families and Community: The Color, Class, and Centrality of Extended Kin Ties. *Sociological Forum, 26*(1), 1-20.

Gordon, L. (2012). Citizenship and the Right to Birth Control. *Dissent (00123846), 59*(4), 60-64.

Hupp, J. M., & Sloutsky, V. M. (2011). Learning to Learn: From Within-Modality to Cross-Modality Transfer During Infancy. *Journal Of Experimental Child Psychology, 110*(3), 408-421.

Joffe, V., Black, E., Oetting, J., & Fujiki, M. (2012). Social, Emotional, and Behavioral Functioning of Secondary School Students With Low Academic and Language Performance: Perspectives From Students, Teachers, and Parents. *Language, Speech & Hearing Services In Schools, 43*(4), 461-473.

Kann, L., O'Malley Olsen, E., McManus, T., Kinchen, S., Chyen, D., Harris, W. A., & ... Centers for Disease Control and Prevention (2011). Sexual Identity, Sex of Sexual Contacts, and Health-Risk Behaviors Among Students in Grades 9-12--Youth Risk Behavior Surveillance, Selected Sites, United States, 2001-2009. Morbidity and Mortality Weekly Report. Early Release. Volume 60. *Centers For Disease Control And Prevention.*

Keaton, P., & National Center for Education Statistics (2012). Numbers and Types of Public Elementary and Secondary Schools from the Common Core of Data: School Year 2010-11. First Look. NCES 2012-325. *National Center For Education Statistics.*

Kern, N., Thukral, R., Ziebarth, T., & National Alliance for Public Charter, S. (2012). A Mission to Serve: How Public Charter Schools Are Designed to Meet the Diverse Demands of Our Communities. Issue Brief. *National Alliance For Public Charter Schools.*

Klein, J., Cornell, D., & Konold, T. (2012). Relationships Between Bullying, School Climate, and Student Risk Behaviors. *School Psychology Quarterly, 27*(3).

Laurie, T., & Stark, H. (n.d). Reconsidering kinship: Beyond the nuclear family with Deleuze and Guattari. *Cultural Studies Review, 18*(1), 19.

Levin, H., & McEwan, P. (2001). *Cost-Effectiveness Analysis*. Thousand Oaks: Sage Publications.

Lichtenstein, N. (2006). *American Capitalism: Social Thought and Political Economy in the Twentieth Century / edited by Nelson Lichtenstein.* Philadelphia : University of Pennsylvania Press, c2006.

Marasco, K. (2011). Creating School Communities through Music. *Online Submission*

Marchant, G. J., University of Colorado at Boulder, E., & Arizona State University, E. (2010). Review of "The Shaping of the American Mind: The Diverging Influences of the College Degree & Civic Learning on American Beliefs." *Education And The Public Interest Center,*

Massey, D., Charles, C., Lundy, G., & Fischer, M. (2003). *The Source of the River: The Social Origins of Freshmen at America's Selective Colleges and Universities.* Princeton: Princeton University Press.

Miller, R. T., & Center for American, P. (2011). Redefining Teacher Pensions: Strategically Defined Benefits for New Teachers and Fiscal Sustainability for All. *Center For American Progress.*

National Center for Education Statistics (ED) (2012). *Supplemental Tables to the NCES Report. Arts Education in Public Elementary and Secondary Schools: 1999-2000 and 2009-10 (NCES 2012-014).* National Center for Education Statistics.

Parsad, B., Spiegelman, M., & National Center for Education Statistics, (2011). A Snapshot of Arts Education in Public Elementary and

Secondary Schools: 2009-10. First Look. NCES 2011-078. *National Center For Education Statistics,*

Parsad, B., Spiegelman, M., & National Center for Education Statistics (2012). Arts Education in Public Elementary and Secondary Schools: 1999-2000 and 2009-10. NCES 2012-014. *National Center For Education Statistics.*

Pedro, J. Y., Miller, R., & Bray, P. (2012). Teacher Knowledge and Dispositions towards Parents and Families: Rethinking Influences and Education of Early Childhood Pre-Service Teachers. *Forum On Public Policy Online, 2012*(1).

Peterson, R. A., Albaum, G. S., & Kozmetsky, G. (1990). *Modern American Capitalism: Understanding Public Attitudes and Perceptions / Robert A. Peterson, Gerald Albaum, and George Kozmetsky.* New York : Quorum Books, 1990.

Picciano, A. (2011). *Educational Leadership and Planning for Technology.* Boston: Pearson.

Ravitch, D. (2000). *Left Back: A Century of Battles Over School Reform.* New York: Touchstone.

Saegert, S., Fields, D., & Libman, K. (2011). Mortgage Foreclosure and Health Disparities: Serial Displacement as Asset Extraction in African American Populations. *Journal Of Urban Health, 88*(3), 390-402.

Sazon, M. C., & National Alliance for Public Charter, S. (2011). Making Room for New Public Schools: How Innovative School Districts Are Learning to Share Public Education Facilities with Charter Schools. *National Alliance For Public Charter Schools.*

Schuler, A., Scheiter, K., Rummer, R., & Gerjets, P. (2012). Explaining the Modality Effect in Multimedia Learning: Is It Due to a Lack of Temporal Contiguity with Written Text and Pictures? *Learning And Instruction, 22*(2), 92-102.

Thelin, J. R. (2004). *A History of American Higher Education.* Baltimore: The Johns Hopkins University Press.

Thurlow, M. L., Vang, M., Cormier, D., & National Center on Educational, O. (2010). Earning a High School Diploma through Alternative Routes. Synthesis Report 76. *National Center On Educational Outcomes, University Of Minnesota.*

Tough, P. (2008). *Whatever It Takes.* New York: Mariner Books.

Tyack, D., & Cuban, L. (1995). *Tinkering Toward Utopia.* Cambridge: Harvard University Press.

US Senate. Committee on Health, E. (2011). *ESEA Reauthorization: The Importance of a World-Class K-12 Education for Our Economic Success. Hearing of the Committee on Health, Education, Labor, and Pensions, United States Senate, One Hundred Eleventh Congress, Second Session on Examining Elementary and Secondary Education Act (ESEA) Reauthorization, Focusing on K-12 Education for Economic Success (March 9, 2010). Senate Hearing 111-885.* US Senate.

Volkman, B. K. (1996). Parent Involvement in Typical Classroom Lessons: Changing Attitudes toward School.

Weller, C. E., & Center for American, P. (2011). Buyer Beware: The Risks to Teacher Effectiveness from Changing Retirement Benefits. *Center For American Progress.*

Winters, M. A. (2012). Measuring the Effect of Charter Schools on Public School Student Achievement in an Urban Environment: Evidence from New York City. *Economics Of Education Review, 31*(2), 293-301.

Wise, C. S. (1993, May 1). Parent and Teacher Attitudes: An Examination of Parent and Teacher Attitudes toward Developmentally Appropriate and Traditional Instructional Practice.

Zorea, A. W. (2012). *Birth control / Aharon W. Zorea.* Santa Barbara, Calif.: Greenwood, c2012.

www.ingramcontent.com/pod-product-compliance
Lightning Source LLC
Chambersburg PA
CBHW021545290526
45785CB00004BA/1526